FIREPLACES AND
WOOD STOVES

TIME
LIFE ®
BOOKS

Other Publications:

LIBRARY OF HEALTH
CLASSICS OF THE OLD WEST
THE EPIC OF FLIGHT
THE GOOD COOK
THE SEAFARERS
THE ENCYCLOPEDIA OF COLLECTIBLES
THE GREAT CITIES
WORLD WAR II
THE WORLD'S WILD PLACES
THE TIME-LIFE LIBRARY OF BOATING
HUMAN BEHAVIOR
THE ART OF SEWING
THE OLD WEST
THE EMERGENCE OF MAN
THE AMERICAN WILDERNESS
THE TIME-LIFE ENCYCLOPEDIA OF GARDENING
LIFE LIBRARY OF PHOTOGRAPHY
THIS FABULOUS CENTURY
FOODS OF THE WORLD
TIME-LIFE LIBRARY OF AMERICA
TIME-LIFE LIBRARY OF ART
GREAT AGES OF MAN
LIFE SCIENCE LIBRARY
THE LIFE HISTORY OF THE UNITED STATES
TIME READING PROGRAM
LIFE NATURE LIBRARY
LIFE WORLD LIBRARY
FAMILY LIBRARY:
   HOW THINGS WORK IN YOUR HOME
   THE TIME-LIFE BOOK OF THE FAMILY CAR
   THE TIME-LIFE FAMILY LEGAL GUIDE
   THE TIME-LIFE BOOK OF FAMILY FINANCE

HOME REPAIR
AND IMPROVEMENT

FIREPLACES AND WOOD STOVES

BY THE EDITORS OF
TIME-LIFE BOOKS

TIME-LIFE BOOKS
ALEXANDRIA, VIRGINIA

Time-Life Books Inc.
is a wholly owned subsidiary of
TIME INCORPORATED

Founder Henry R. Luce 1898-1967

Editor-in-Chief Henry Anatole Grunwald
President J. Richard Munro
Chairman of the Board Ralph P. Davidson
Executive Vice President Clifford J. Grum
Chairman, Executive Committee James R. Shepley
Editorial Director Ralph Graves
Group Vice President, Books Joan D. Manley
Vice Chairman Arthur Temple

TIME-LIFE BOOKS INC.

Managing Editor Jerry Korn
Executive Editor David Maness
Assistant Managing Editors Dale M. Brown (planning), George Constable, Martin Mann, John Paul Porter, Gerry Schremp (acting)
Art Director Tom Suzuki
Chief of Research David L. Harrison
Director of Photography Robert G. Mason
Assistant Art Director Arnold C. Holeywell
Assistant Chief of Research Carolyn L. Sackett
Assistant Director of Photography Dolores A. Littles

Chairman John D. McSweeney
President Carl G. Jaeger
Executive Vice Presidents John Steven Maxwell, David J. Walsh
Vice Presidents George Artandi (comptroller); Stephen L. Bair (legal counsel); Peter G. Barnes; Nicholas Benton (public relations); John L. Canova; Beatrice T. Dobie (personnel); Carol Flaumenhaft (consumer affairs); James L. Mercer (Europe/South Pacific); Herbert Sorkin (production); Paul R. Stewart (marketing)

HOME REPAIR AND IMPROVEMENT

Editorial Staff for Fireplaces and Wood Stoves

Editor Robert M. Jones
Assistant Editors Betsy Frankel, Brooke Stoddard
Designer Edward Frank
Picture Editor Adrian Allen
Text Editors Peter Pocock (senior), Lynn R. Addison, Robert A. Doyle
Staff Writers Patricia C. Bangs, Jan Leslie Cook, Rachel Cox, Steven J. Forbis, Kathleen M. Kiely, Victoria W. Monks, Kirk Y. Saunders, Ania Savage, Mary-Sherman Willis
Researcher Marilyn Murphy
Art Associates George Bell, Fred Holz, Lorraine Rivard, Peter Simmons
Editorial Assistant Susan Larson

Editorial Production

Production Editor Douglas B. Graham
Operations Manager Gennaro C. Esposito, Gordon E. Buck (assistant)
Assistant Production Editor Feliciano Madrid
Quality Control Robert L. Young (director), James J. Cox (assistant), Daniel J. McSweeney, Michael G. Wight (associates)
Art Coordinator Anne B. Landry
Copy Staff Susan B. Galloway (chief), Diane Ullius Jarrett, Celia Beattie
Picture Department Betsy Donahue
Traffic Kimberly K. Lewis

Correspondents: Elisabeth Kraemer (Bonn); Margot Hapgood, Dorothy Bacon, Lesley Coleman (London); Susan Jonas, Lucy T. Voulgaris (New York); Maria Vincenza Aloisi, Josephine du Brusle (Paris); Ann Natanson (Rome). Valuable assistance was also provided by: Judy Aspinall, Karin B. Pearce (London); Carolyn T. Chubet, Miriam Hsia, Christina Lieberman (New York); Mimi Murphy (Rome).

THE CONSULTANTS: Roswell W. Ard is a consulting structural engineer and a professional home inspector in northern Michigan. He has written professionally on the structural uses of wood and on wood-frame construction techniques.

Morris Katz, Vice President of Acme Stove Co., Inc., has been in the fireplace and wood-stove business for more than four decades. Richard Kimmel works with Mr. Katz in his Washington, D.C., concern.

Harris Mitchell, special consultant for Canada, has worked in the field of home repair and improvement for more than two decades. He is Homes editor of *Today* magazine and author of a syndicated newspaper column, "You Wanted to Know," as well as a number of books on home improvement.

Donald D. Sager worked as a mason for more than two decades before becoming dean of the Charles S. Monroe Vocational Technical Center in Leesburg, Virginia. Lyle E. Wilt, an instructor at the school, is a bricklayer by trade, with more than two decades of construction and teaching experience.

Dr. Jay W. Shelton, Director of Shelton Energy Research in Santa Fe, New Mexico, is the author of *Wood Heat Safety* and *Woodburner's Encyclopedia*.

Winston Whitney, who operates a chimney-cleaning business in the Washington, D.C., area, is trained in stone and brick masonry and has designed and built his own fireplaces. He has also done research on fire hazards for the Safety Office of the Washington, D.C., Fire Department.

For information about any Time-Life book, please write:
Reader Information
Time-Life Books
541 North Fairbanks Court
Chicago, Illinois 60611

Library of Congress Cataloguing in Publication Data
Main entry under title:
Fireplaces and wood stoves.
   (Home repair and improvement; 28)
   Includes index.
   1. Fireplaces. 2. Stoves, Wood.
   I. Time-Life Books. II. Series.
TH7425.F58   697'. 04   81-5771
ISBN 0-8094-2444-4   AACR2
ISBN 0-8094-2443-6 (lib. bdg.)
ISBN 0-8094-2442-8 (ret. ed.)

Contents

New lease on life. A brand-new body, custom-made by a sheet-metal fabricator, rejuvenates this turn-of-the-century wood stove. The stove's original cast-iron fittings—a finely detailed door and a base with curved legs—are attached to the new body with stove bolts, the coarsely threaded fasteners that were originally designed for precisely this purpose.

An old English proverb says: "A fair fire does a room make gay." In a time of fearsome fuel bills and uncertain supplies, a wood fire can also supply considerably more than merriment. Having a fireplace or a wood stove that is capable of generating a substantial portion of your household heat can also make you feel secure and even a little smug.

The choice of installations, whether ready-made or custom-constructed, is enormous. No other significant element of house design is available in such a variety of sizes, shapes, styles and materials. Making a decision among them will require thoughtful compromises involving a number of technical considerations: how much heat will be needed, how often, in what kind of physical space, to be vented by what means. But allowance will also have to be made for such factors as the existence of a usable chimney, the architectural character and social function of the room, and the psychological effect intended. Only then can the full potential of a fireplace or a stove be realized.

Behind the great variety of choices in fireplace and stove design lies a long history of attempts to improve heating efficiency. The standard 18th Century fireplace, with its huge opening and its damperless flue, was notorious for producing a blast of radiant heat directly in front of the hearth, but sending most of the energy—as much as 90 per cent—straight up the chimney. It also consumed wood at a prodigious rate. Far more efficient was the cast-iron box stove brought to America by German settlers, which provided the inspiration for Benjamin Franklin's Pennsylvania Fire-Place. But even Franklin's invention, with its baffled heat chambers and cold-air intake, is no match for modern slow-burning, airtight cast-iron stoves, which are designed to extract the greatest amount of heat from the least amount of wood.

Fireplaces, too, have come a long way, thanks in part to the genius of one of Franklin's contemporaries, Benjamin Thompson, an expatriate American who became Count Rumford. In the late 18th Century, Rumford designed a fireplace that was distinguished for its relatively shallow hearth, small opening and even smaller fireback—all of which had the combined effect of projecting a considerably larger share of the fire's heat back into the room. Rumford's design is still used today for many masonry fireplaces, and it is the model for an array of metal fireplaces—boxlike inserts that improve the heating efficiency of both new and old masonry fireplaces. Fitted with elaborate venting systems and even auxiliary blowers that further improve its heat delivery, the modern-day fireplace practically guarantees a "fair fire."

Extracting the Most Heat from a Wood Fire

The warmth of a wood fire has long been a source of physical and psychological pleasure, but in recent years, as the costs of other heating fuels have soared, wood heat has also been regarded as a possible way to save money. For many people the experiment has been disappointing. They have discovered that a fireplace or a wood stove can be inefficient, troublesome and sometimes downright dangerous to operate.

Such problems usually arise from a failure to understand how an open fire affects the flow of air through a house or from faulty design in the fireplace or stove—design that fails to take advantage of the chemistry of burning wood. Properly handled, wood heat is both safe and efficient—an excellent and entirely feasible way to warm parts of the house, permitting you to close off unused rooms and turn down the thermostat.

All stoves and fireplaces, no matter what fuel they burn, operate on the same basic principles. Oxygen in the air feeds the fire in the firebox; the fire, in turn, warms the air passing over it. The warmed air expands, becomes less dense and rises up the chimney or stovepipe. As the warm air rises, cool air replaces it, thus ensuring a plentiful supply of oxygen in the firebox. This process is called convection. Heat is meanwhile being absorbed by the metal or masonry firebox, and is radiated back into the room or conducted into the room through the walls of the firebox. Either way, additional warmth is supplied to the house.

The efficiency of a stove or a fireplace depends largely on its receiving enough oxygen for combustion without at the same time sending too much heat up the flue. Although air is only about one-fifth oxygen by volume, the strong convection current created by the large opening of most fireplaces draws in enough air to supply 7 to 10 times as much oxygen as the fire needs to burn. The bulk of this heated air escapes up the flue, reducing the heating efficiency of an average fireplace to about 10 per cent.

This strong convection current has another disagreeable consequence. The steady flow of air up the chimney causes colder outdoor air to seep into the house to replace it, triggering the thermostat of the central heating system and raising rather than lowering heating bills.

Over the years, alterations in fireplace design have improved the balance between heat loss and heat gain. The fireplace with a shallow firebox, shown on page 10, is one of the oldest solutions, dating back to the 1600s. It radiates more heat into the room, boosting heating efficiency as high as 15 to 18 per cent. Another solution is the modern circulating fireplace shown on page 10, which directs heated air back into the room, salvaging much of the fire's heat output.

No fireplace, however, can match the efficiency of a wood stove, which is specifically designed to control the manner in which wood burns. A wood fire, though it may seem an utterly random event, actually progresses through predictable stages, as the pictures on page 10 show. In the initial stages, while the temperature is rising and the flow of oxygen is being established, the fire needs pampering. Later, when coals have been formed and the fire is hottest, its heating potential must be exploited.

A wood stove is ideally suited for handling these tasks. It can be made airtight and, with strategically placed vents and dampers, can precisely control the flow of air in and out of the firebox. In fact, a modern wood stove can reach an efficiency of 60 to 70 per cent—comparable to that of a fuel-oil furnace.

Other factors of heating efficiency are the placement and length of the chimney or stovepipe. The best position for a chimney is in the center of a house. There the flue stays warmer, promoting convection, and the heat conducted through the flue walls becomes available. In addition—within reasonable limits—the taller the chimney, the longer the column of warm air inside and the stronger the pull, or draft. A chimney that is very tall, however, may not draw well because the air inside cools before it reaches the top.

To complicate matters, the proportions of other fireplace dimensions also affect efficiency. The firebox opening may be too large, or the chimney throat too small, for the volume of air passing through; if these proportions are off, air backs up and reduces the draft. Although there is no established ratio for these proportions, the chart on page 70 will help you increase the efficiency of your fireplace or design an efficient new one.

Finally, before making any decisions about heating with wood, analyze the way warm air will flow through your house. Single-level houses may require more than one heating unit, but houses with more than one floor can often be heated with a central stove or hearth. As illustrated in the drawings (right), upstairs rooms can be warmed by air rising from below by convection; ducts, fans and floor or wall registers will help distribute the warm air, sending some of it back to the lower floor.

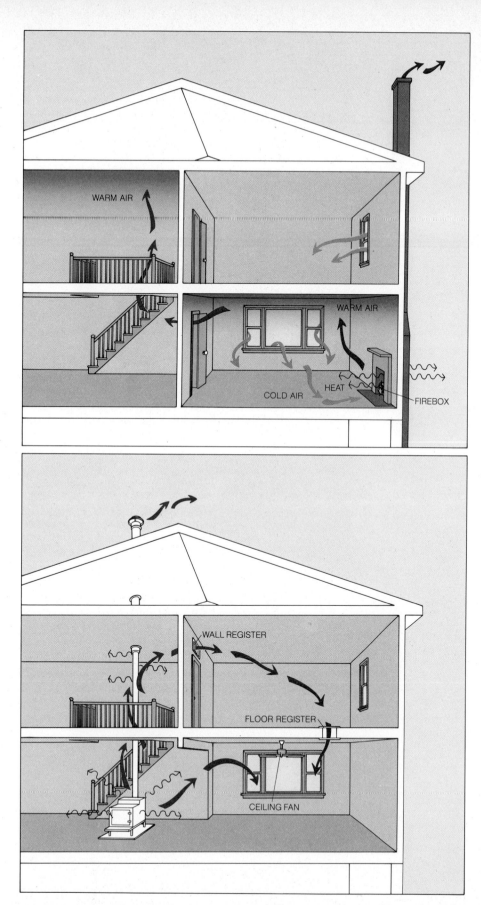

WARM AIR

WARM AIR

COLD AIR

HEAT

FIREBOX

WALL REGISTER

FLOOR REGISTER

CEILING FAN

Counteracting Drawbacks in Heat Distribution

The chilling effects of a fireplace fire. As this diagrammatic drawing of the movement of air through a typical house shows, the warmth provided by a fireplace can come to some unwanted ends. When a fire is first lighted in the fireplace, the air it needs for combustion is drawn from elsewhere in the house and from the outdoors, through tiny cracks around doors and windows. This creates cold drafts. As the air passes over the fire, it warms and rises up the chimney, carrying some of the fire's heat with it. At the same time the heat radiated by the fire itself, which can reach a temperature as high as 2,000° F., warms the air in front of the hearth—or it may be conducted through the back wall of the fireplace and be lost outdoors. Meanwhile, the warm air within the room rises and pools against the ceiling, leaving a layer of cooler air below. At the door the warm air escapes and travels up the stair well, where it pools again on the upstairs hall ceiling. There it is blocked from entering upstairs rooms by the wall above the upstairs door, though the door is open.

Measures that combat heat loss. If the heat source—in this case a stove—is located in the center of the house near the stair well, all the heat produced by the stove and its stovepipe can be conserved and circulated indoors. Weatherstripping on doors and window blocks cold air from the outside, cutting down one source of drafts; the stove's closed firebox and controllable air intake limit drafts generated by the fire.

To improve the dispersal of warm air through this house, part of a wall on the ground floor was removed, and a large ceiling fan was added. The fan, which can also be used for cooling in summer, spins at a very slow speed, forcing down the warm air that collects at the ceiling.

To warm the upstairs rooms, wall and floor registers were installed. The registers have louvered openings, which can be closed if desired. The wall register, above the door, allows the pooled warm air in the stair well to enter the room even when the door is shut. The floor register, near a corner of the room, allows warm air from the ground floor to rise by convection when the ceiling fan is off. When the fan is on, the floor register acts as a return vent for air set in motion and circulated through the house by the fan.

How Wood Burns, from Kindling to Ash

The three stages of combustion. When a fire is started, the logs are brought to a temperature of 200° to 500° by a kindling fire of newspaper and twigs *(below, left)*. In this first stage, the logs begin to smoke—giving off steam, tar and volatile gases such as carbon monoxide, methane and hydrogen. Pulled by the draft of the kindling fire, the smoke rises up the chimney.

During the second stage of combustion, long yellow, red-tipped flames begin to appear from the underside of the logs *(below, center)*. When the fire is at this stage, given sufficient oxygen, the temperature of the wood increases from 600° to 1,000°—hot enough that it will sustain a fire without the help of kindling. Meanwhile, as the temperature inside the firebox rises from 1,000° to 1,200°, the volatile gases in the smoke ignite. These gases contain roughly half the wood's potential heat; they burn at temperatures of about 1,100° and give off bursts of hot blue flame.

When the wood temperature reaches 900° or more, coals begin to form on the underside of the logs *(below, right)*, producing small, hot blue flames and little smoke. This is the third stage of combustion. When the logs are turned over, they will fragment into chunks of glowing orange-red coals, and these coals contain the other half of the wood's heat potential. As the coals burn, they turn first into black charcoal, then into gray, powdery ash—this is the uncombustible residue of the fire.

Fireplaces Designed to Maximize Heat

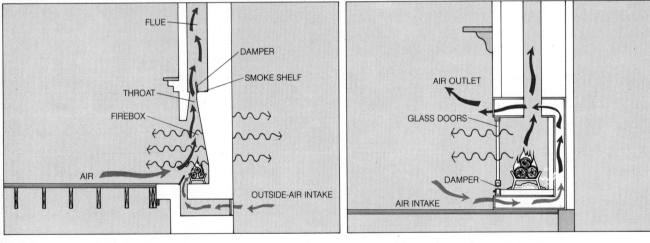

A firebox that fights heat loss. The wide, shallow firebox of this fireplace radiates heat back into the room. An air intake, underneath the firebox, draws outdoor air into the fire through a hinged opening on the floor of the firebox. The air feeds the fire, then rises up the tapering firebox throat, past the damper, into the flue. The damper, a metal trap door in front of the smoke shelf, controls the chimney's draw; it can be adjusted to enlarge or reduce the size of the opening into the flue, thus regulating the suction, or draft, created by the air that fans the fire. The damper can also be closed entirely, to prevent cold air from entering the room at times when the fireplace is not being used.

A cavity that generates warm air. Designed to heat by convection, a circulating fireplace draws in cold air through a floor-level vent and carries it through a space around the firebox, expelling the warmed air through vents at the top. Many circulating fireplaces have glass doors, which help reduce heat waste while they contain heat in the firebox to warm the air flowing around it. The air needed for combustion passes through a damper at the base of the doors; the damper can be adjusted to regulate the amount of air and control the rate at which the fire burns. The chimney's draw is also reduced, providing enough air for a good draft but siphoning less room heat outdoors.

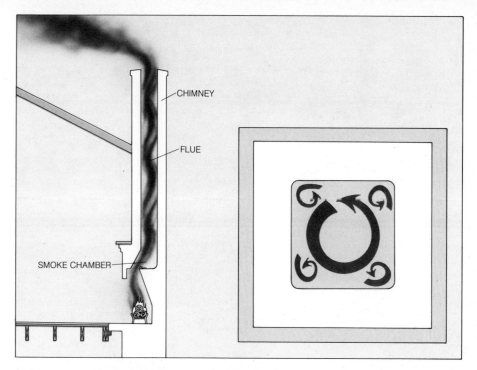

CHIMNEY

FLUE

SMOKE CHAMBER

Tracking the path of a draft. When a fire ignites, smoke and hot air from the firebox rise past the open damper into the smoke chamber. From there the smoke and hot air follow a spiraling upward path, gradually warming and reversing cold downdrafts from the mouth of the chimney. Until this pattern is established, the broad smoke chamber and narrow flue opening help prevent descending gusts of cold air from pushing smoke back into the room.

A chimney's shape and interior surface can affect its draft. Some experts believe that the column of rising air, because of its spiraling path, flows more easily in cylindrical chimneys. Since most clay flue liners are square or rectangular to make them easier to install, however, smoke eddies and collects in their corners *(inset),* slowing the air flow. Similarly, a flue thickly coated with soot or creosote, or an old chimney whose flue sections are connected with rough mortar joints, will cause the rising smoke to drag against the flue walls; the most efficient chimneys are those that have smooth mortar joints connecting the sections of the flue liner.

Two Stoves Designed to Hoard Heat

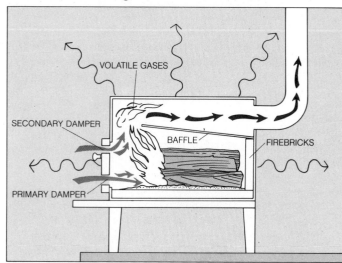

VOLATILE GASES

SECONDARY DAMPER

BAFFLE

FIREBRICKS

PRIMARY DAMPER

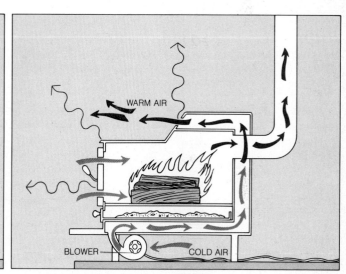

WARM AIR

BLOWER

COLD AIR

Force-feeding the fire. Shaped like a box with legs, this wood-burning stove loads from the front through a tight-fitting door equipped with two dampers. The primary damper supplies air for combustion; the secondary damper provides air to promote ignition of the volatile gases released by the burning logs. The baffle, a large iron plate, extends from the back of the stove almost to the front; it forces the rising gases to the front where, fed by air from the secondary damper, they ignite. The result is more complete combustion of both the wood and the gases.

This stove radiates heat. And the firebricks lining the sides and bottom absorb the fire's heat and release it slowly, even after the fire has died.

A firebox encased in hot air. In addition to radiating heat, this circulating stove also warms by circulating heated air. An air chamber around the firebox pulls in cold air from the room, warms it, and releases it back into the room. Some circulating stoves are equipped with a small electric blower at the air intake to increase the flow of air. And some blowers are equipped with a thermostat, which automatically shuts off the electric blower when the stove cools down.

Safety Precautions to Keep Fire in Its Place

Whenever fire is introduced into a house, it must be treated with great respect. The most immediate hazards of a fireplace or a wood stove are that the fire may escape directly, in the form of hot coals or sparks; that its radiant heat may be great enough to ignite nearby combustible materials; or that flammable residues in the chimney may catch fire and spread to adjacent wood framing or to the roof. All three of these dangers can be virtually eliminated by careful installation and operation of the wood-burning system, plus a regular program of inspection and maintenance.

The installation of a stove or a fireplace will usually be governed by local building and fire codes. These codes often require that the design and materials of a wood stove meet standards set by local authorities or be approved by a recognized agency, such as Underwriters' Laboratories (UL).

Usually, fire codes also provide specific instructions for stove placement. It is important to maintain a safe distance between the fire and nearby walls; wood can ignite at temperatures as low as 200° F.—much less than the 800° temperature radiated by some stoves. Therefore, most codes require protective shields behind and beneath a stove and its flue, to dissipate heat before it reaches combustible wall or floor materials. Most codes also specify the thickness of the masonry in a fireplace and chimney and the amount of air space that is required between the masonry and combustible interior walls.

Regular inspection, cleaning and maintenance (page 120) are the best insurance against chimney fires and fires resulting from damage to a stove or flue. Thoroughly check the entire system before lighting the first fire of the season, and repeat the inspection every month or so.

Proper accessories are needed for the safe operation of any wood-burning system. Andirons or a cradle-shaped grate will keep burning logs from falling or rolling beyond the firebox opening; a metal container provides safe transport of ashes, which may contain hot coals. Every fireplace requires a close-fitting screen or glass doors to prevent sparks and hot coals from popping out.

Safe operation also requires that you pay attention to the fire itself. Stoves should never be allowed to become so hot that the metal glows: Heat this intense can cause dangerous cracks. Burn only the fuels for which a stove is designed, avoiding any substance that could increase the heat of the fire—starter fluids, coal, cardboard and especially trash such as Christmas-tree boughs and plastic wrappings. And never store extra firewood so close to the flames that it might ignite outside the firebox.

If, despite all your precautions, a fire does break out, you can ensure an early warning with properly installed smoke detectors. Heavy smoke is usually the first sign of a spreading fire. Fire officials recommend that at least one smoke detector be placed on each level of a house, especially if a stove is to be left burning overnight or if the coals of an open fire are to be left banked.

The two major types of smoke detector are easily installed and reasonably priced, and can operate with either battery power or house current. Ionization detectors use a cloud of atomic particles to conduct electricity between two terminals; when smoke is present, the flow of current is reduced, triggering the alarm. Photoelectric detectors sound the alarm when smoke particles interrupt a light beam inside the unit.

An ionization detector, because it is particularly sensitive to smoke from clean-burning fires of paper and wood, is the better alarm to install in the sleeping areas of the house, but it may give too many false alarms if it is placed in the same room as a stove or a fireplace. A photoelectric detector, in contrast, reacts more slowly to a clean-burning fire, but its quick response to the heavy smoke of a smoldering fire makes it a better choice for areas near fireplaces or stoves. However, it too can give false alarms, and though the best location would seem to be in the same room as the fire, such a detector should usually be installed in an adjacent room or hall.

Local fire officials often are willing to help you plan the placement of smoke detectors. After they are installed, all smoke detectors should be tested once a month, and cleaned occasionally to keep dust from reducing their sensitivity.

The best response to almost any home fire is to call the fire department and leave the house immediately, but you still should have equipment on hand for fighting small fires that can be quickly controlled (box, opposite). Baking soda or salt can be effective to smother a spark smoldering in a rug. A bucket of damp sand kept near a stove will slow down a fire out of control.

A type ABC multipurpose extinguisher, however, is the best equipment to use for fighting stove and fireplace fires. This kind of extinguisher, which sprays the fire with a dry compound (usually ammonium phosphate), is better than a liquid extinguisher because liquid can cause a stove, chimney or flue to cool so rapidly it cracks; liquid can also injure the user with rebounding steam and ash. Keep at least one ABC extinguisher with a five- to eight-pound capacity near the door of any room that contains a stove or a fireplace, and read its instructions so that you know how to use it. Check its pressure gauge regularly; the gauge should register more than 100 pounds per square inch. If it does not, the extinguisher must be recharged or replaced.

You need an established plan of escape in the event of fire, using regular exits at ground level or emergency ladders from upper floors. Make sure all family members know the plan, and include an assembly point for meeting outside the house so that you will know when everyone has exited safely.

How to Keep a Chimney Fire from Spreading

Although the correct response to any fire larger than a smoldering patch on a rug is to call the fire department, in some cases you may be able to prevent its spread while you wait for the fire trucks to arrive. This is especially true of a chimney fire—easily identified by its sound, much like that of a roaring train—which you will probably be able to keep from spreading to the other parts of the house.

Working about 6 feet from the fireplace and being sure at all times that you have a safe exit behind you, spray the fire in the firebox with your extinguisher in a sweeping back-and-forth motion, coating the flaming logs from the bottom up. The draft from the fire will probably draw some of the chemical up the chimney, where it will help to extinguish the burning creosote or soot that is the cause of the fire. Once the wood in the fireplace is no longer aflame, cut off the air flow to the chimney by closing the damper and sealing the fireplace opening with a piece of sheet metal or gypsum wallboard. Then, working outside, hose down the roof with water to prevent the fire from spreading. Try to avoid spraying the chimney: It might crack.

Fight a fire in a stove flue in the same manner, but be careful when you first open the stove: The sudden release of pressure from within the flue may cause flames to leap from the firebox. Once the fire in the flue is out, close the vents and damper for at least 30 minutes to prevent it from restarting.

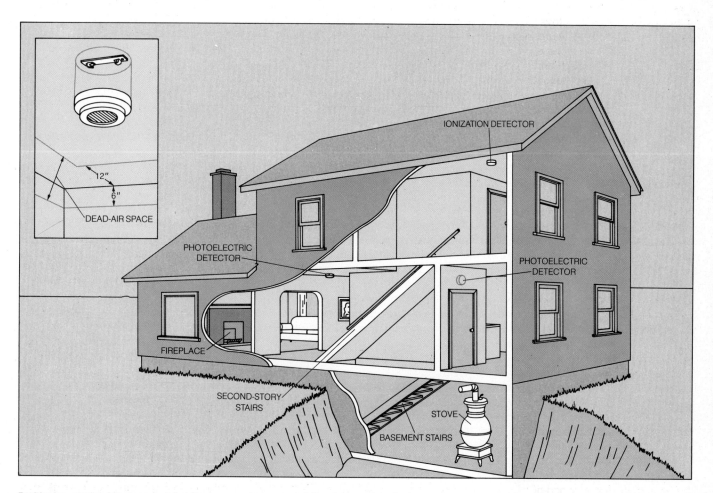

Positioning smoke detectors. Install at least one detector on each floor of the house. On the first floor, position a detector in an area adjacent to any room with a fireplace or a wood stove; to avoid false alarms, use a photoelectric detector for any location where some fumes are normal. If you have a basement fireplace or stove, install a photoelectric unit at the top of the stairs, on the basement side. On other levels of the house, especially outside upstairs bedrooms, use ionization alarms.

Wherever possible, mount a smoke detector on the ceiling, in the center of a room or hall. Avoid placing detectors in dead-air spaces at the corners of the room, where smoke is unlikely to circulate *(inset)*. Ceiling-mounted detectors are most effective when they are placed 12 inches or more from the nearest wall, to avoid the stagnant corners. For the same reason, a wall-mounted unit should be placed 6 inches or more below the ceiling. In a room that has a sloping ceiling, position the detector about 12 inches below the highest point, where smoke will tend to pool. If the ceiling has exposed beams, mount the detector on the bottom of a beam, not in the space between beams.

Upgrading the Performance of a Firebox

The efficiency of a fireplace depends largely on the efficient functioning of the firebox the firebrick floor and the three firebrick walls that surround the fire. Many factors can reduce that efficiency, but most problems fall into two main categories: Either they involve structural damage to the firebricks or to the damper at the top of the firebox, or they result from flaws in the design. Fortunately, most problems are easily solved.

Over the years the structural elements of any firebox that is used regularly are bound to deteriorate. The combination of heat from fires and moisture that condenses on the chimney and trickles down into the firebox can cause damper parts to rust and break, and mortar joints between the firebricks to crumble.

If the damper frame breaks, you may need professional help; the frame is usually anchored in the masonry. Alternatively, you can abandon the existing damper by removing the plate, and substitute a chimney-top damper (page 22).

Usually, however, the broken part is the handle, or one or more of the cotter pins that join the damper's movable parts. If the handle breaks, simply remove the plate and handle and take them to a building- or masonry-supply store for replacement. When you buy new cotter pins, be sure they are stainless steel, and buy pins slightly smaller than the holes they will fit, to allow for heat expansion.

Crumbling mortar joints between the firebricks are easy to repair, too. All you need do is scrape out the mortar with an old chisel and press special fireplace mortar into the joints with a mason's tuck pointer or—if the brand of mortar you buy is in a tube—with a caulking gun. You may also want to install a chimney cap to keep the rain out (page 22).

If a fireplace functions inefficiently because of the firebox design, a remedy is likely to be more complicated. To some extent, accessories sold by fireplace-equipment dealers can be used to make a fireplace throw more heat into the room. A circulating grate of hollow C-shaped tubes, for example, will draw in room-temperature air at the bottom and return it as warm air at the top. Another accessory, called a fireback, is a decorative cast-iron plate that is mounted on the back wall of the firebox to absorb heat and radiate it into the room.

If the design problem involves either inadequate air intake or faulty draft, correcting it takes even more planning and effort. Air intake, in particular, has become a problem as houses have become better insulated and more tightly built. Drafty Victorian mansions allowed more than enough outside air to seep in around windows and doors to feed the fire. Today, energy-conscious homeowners seal every crack, a measure that can cause a fire to die of oxygen starvation.

The solution is to create passageways that will bring outdoor air directly into the firebox. Ideally, there should be two passages, one through each side wall into the firebox. Since the firebox side walls are angled, it might be necessary to break through not only the firebox and its liner, but also a layer of masonry filler before you reach the outside chimney wall. (If the distance from a side wall to the outside is more than 18 inches, it may be easier to cut one hole for a 4-inch pipe through the back wall.)

To cut a 2½-inch hole through masonry, you will need to rent a hammer drill and two ¼-inch bits from a tool-rental store. One bit should be 4 inches long; the other should be the longest available, usually 19 inches. For digging through the loosened brick and filler, you will need a 1-foot-long mason's chisel or a 16-inch length of ½-inch reinforcing bar, sharpened to a chisel edge at one end; a metal shop will do the sharpening.

To line the passageways, you will need galvanized pipe 2 inches in diameter, available at plumbing-supply stores. Order it after the passageways are cleared, so that you can obtain a precise measurement. Each pipe should be threaded at one end to receive a cap that will cover the inside opening when the fireplace is not being used.

Faulty draft, another problem related to firebox design, is one of the things that cause a fireplace to smoke. The difficulty occurs when the flue is not large enough or the chimney is too short in relation to the size of the front firebox opening. As a result, the flow of air up the chimney is not strong enough to pull up all the smoke generated by the fire.

You can, of course, increase the draft by extending the chimney (pages 20-21). But there also are two ways to improve the draft at firebox level. One way is to install glass doors, which let you regulate the air flow and also reduce the loss of heated air up the chimney. The second way is to decrease the size of the firebox opening by lowering the fireplace lintel with added courses of brick.

If you choose the latter solution, first experiment with aluminum foil (page 17) to determine exactly how far the lintel must be lowered. If one brick course is enough to solve the problem, drill out 4 inches of mortar from beneath the first brick at the top of each side of the opening, making two slots. Then slide the ends of a length of flat iron, ¼ inch thick and 3 inches wide, into the slots. After setting 2-by-4 props temporarily under it, use this iron band as the base for an added course of bricks, laid end to end; fill the long joint between the new bricks and the old lintel with mortar.

But if your test indicates that the lintel should be lowered by more than one brick course, you will need to install a new L-shaped lintel as a base for as many new brick courses as needed. For this procedure, it is important that you have everything at hand before you start to work; the support for the existing lintel will be weakened for a short time, and you must work quickly. Order a 3-inch-wide angle iron of ¼-inch steel. Have it cut 6 to 8 inches longer than the width of the finished fireplace opening.

A simpler and less expensive, but more obtrusive, way to lower the lintel is to install a hood of 24-gauge black iron, available at sheet-metal shops, across the top of the firebox opening. Such a hood should be cut long enough to span the opening and should be twice as deep as the amount by which the lintel is to be lowered. It is then folded lengthwise, into an L shape, and glued to the underside of the existing lintel with heat-resistant silicone adhesive. An even simpler solution is to raise the hearth by adding one or more layers of firebrick, cut to fit snugly against the slanted firebox walls. These firebricks need not be mortared; but they will, of course, be visible above the outer hearth.

Dismantling a Broken Damper for Repair

Variations on a common design. A typical damper consists of a frame, which rests on top of the firebox walls, and various interconnected parts that are designed to pivot in unison, thereby adjusting the position of the damper plate. The movement of the damper plate controls the size of the opening between the firebox and the smoke chamber, which is directly above

it. One side of the damper frame has an angled lip against which the damper plate closes, creating a silhouette that resembles a peaked roof. In one kind of damper *(top inset)*, there are three movable parts—the damper plate, a ratcheted arm and a handle. Another kind *(bottom inset)* has only two movable parts, the damper plate and a ratcheted handle.

Any of a damper's movable parts can deteriorate, as can the cotter pins that fasten them together. To remove the parts and pins for replacement on the first version, use pliers to remove the cotter pins. To disassemble the second version, remove the screw that holds the handle bracket to the frame, then pull out the cotter pin that connects the handle to the damper plate.

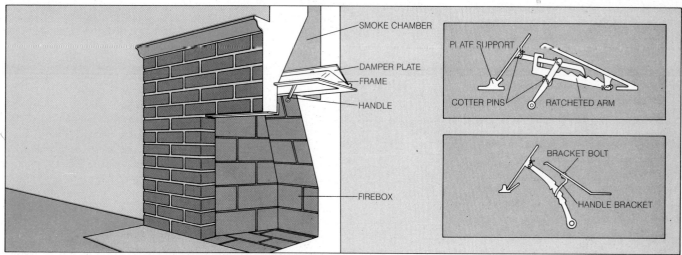

Improving the Draft with Glass Doors

1 Positioning the frame. Attach the mounting brackets and lintel clamps to the top of the glass-screen frame, using the bolts provided. Then tilt the top of the frame away from you so that you can slip the lintel clamps beneath the lintel, and push the bottom of the frame into position; the top and sides will be flat against the face of the fireplace, overlapping the bricks. If fiberglass insulation protrudes around the edges, use a putty knife to push it back out of sight.

2 Anchoring the frame in place. Adjust the sliding lintel clamps on the brackets until both fit snugly under the lintel, then use a wrench to tighten the pressure bolt against the lintel.

If your frame has bottom brackets, drill holes in the firebox floor for lead anchors before you fasten the frame top. Insert the anchors, slide the frame in, tighten the top bolts; fasten the bottom brackets with the screws that are provided.

Cutting Air Passageways
to Give a Fire More Oxygen

1 Establishing the pipe locations. Lay a carpenter's framing square on the firebox floor, with the long arm perpendicular to the back wall and extending through the front opening, and the corner touching a side wall of the firebox. Position the square so that the long arm projects into the firebox 3 inches more than the thickness of the fireplace jamb plus the thickness of the house wall *(inset)*—the easiest place to measure the thickness of the house wall is at an open window. Mark the point where the square touches the firebox wall, measure up 5 inches and make a mark; center a compass on the mark, and swing a circle with a 2½-inch diameter. Mark a circle on the opposite side wall in the same way. Score the perimeter of each circle with a cold chisel and a small sledge hammer.

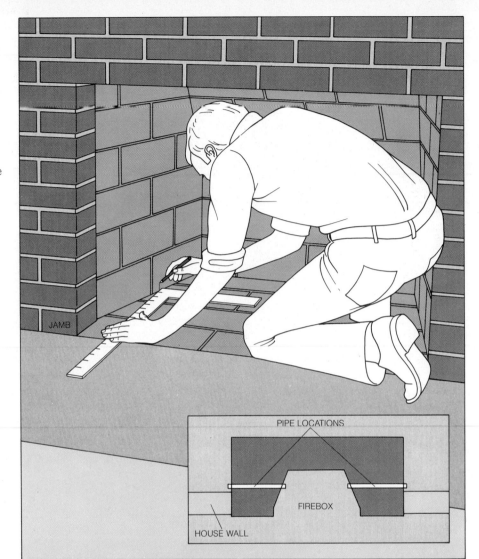

PIPE LOCATIONS

FIREBOX

HOUSE WALL

JAMB

2 Boring the starter holes. Lay a protective cloth or plastic sheet over the firebox floor and outer hearth, put on goggles and gloves, and drill a hole into the center of one of the circles, using a hammer drill fitted with a 4-inch-long bit. Switch to a 19-inch-long bit and, with the power off, insert the bit into the hole; turn on the power and bore through the outer chimney wall. Drill a similar hole in the other circle.

Put the 4-inch-long bit back in the hammer drill, and bore three or four additional holes within each 2½-inch circle to further loosen the masonry. Then use a small sledge hammer and a cold chisel to clean as much debris as possible from each hole. Repeat from the outside, to clear holes through the outer chimney wall.

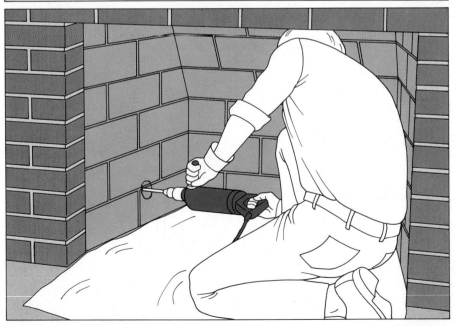

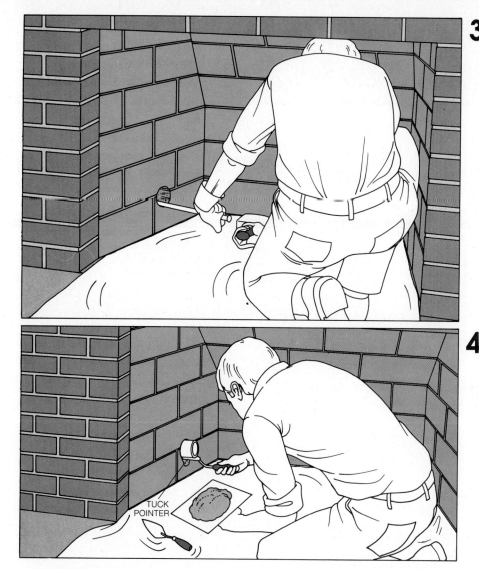

3 **Digging out the passageways.** Using a 16-inch length of reinforcing rod ground to a chisel edge at one end or a mason's chisel, clear out any rubble between the holes in the firebox and the chimney walls. Working alternately from inside and outside the house, push the sharp end of the rod into a hole and tap the blunt end with a small sledge to loosen any masonry and mortar between the chimney and firebox walls.

When both passageways are opened to a 2½-inch diameter, measure their lengths with a steel tape; then add 4 inches to each measurement. Get two pieces of 2-inch-diameter galvanized-steel pipe cut, one to each of these sizes, and order them threaded at one end. Buy a threaded cap for each pipe. Push the pipes into the passageways, threaded ends far enough inside the firebox to keep the caps from scraping the walls when they are screwed into place.

4 **Wedging the pipes in place.** To anchor each pipe firmly in its passageway, push brick chips into the holes in the firebox wall and the chimney wall. At the firebox end of the passageway, push as much fireplace mortar as possible into the brick chips and around the pipe, using the tip of a mason's tuck pointer; then, with a small pointing trowel, smooth the mortar flush with the firebrick. Outside, patch the area around each pipe in the same way, but use brick mortar.

Clean out debris that may have got into the pipes. Then cut two 2-inch-round pieces of ½-inch mesh hardware cloth and push the disks into the open pipe ends outside the house, to keep small animals from using the passageways.

TUCK POINTER

Reducing the Size of the Firebox Opening

1 **Establishing a new lintel height.** Cut a sheet of aluminum foil slightly longer than the width of the firebox opening; tape the foil across the chimney breast just above the lintel, allowing it to overhang the fireplace opening a distance equal to one brick course. Light a smoky fire in the firebox (newspapers and dry leaves produce more smoke than wood does). If no smoke escapes into the room, lower the lintel height only one brick course, using a piece of flat iron and the method described on page 14. If a single course of bricks fails to stop the smoking, lower the foil a distance equal to two brick courses; if smoke still escapes, a distance of three courses. Leave the foil in position through several fires, to check the adjustment.

2 Cutting into the jambs. Brace the existing steel lintel with two 2-by-4s, cutting them exactly to length and wedging them between the lintel and the firebox floor. Starting at the top of the fireplace opening, remove the bricks or half-bricks on both sides of the opening for the number of courses the opening must be reduced in this example, two. To remove the bricks, loosen the mortar in the joints by drilling several holes into each joint with a ¼-inch bit; then chip away the remaining mortar with a cold chisel and a small sledge hammer until you can pull out the bricks. Scrape any remaining mortar from the exposed surfaces of bricks left in place, using the cold chisel and the sledge hammer.

3 Installing the new lintel: Before setting the new lintel into the openings in the jambs, spread a layer of brick mortar over the top of the exposed bricks in each opening; use enough mortar to match the thickness of the existing mortar joints. Then carefully remove the 2-by-4 braces, and slide the new lintel into place; for an L-shaped lintel, position the lintel with the vertical leg facing the rear, and the front edge ½ inch back from the faces of the bricks. Work quickly; the original lintel now has little support. Press the new lintel into the mortar so that the mortar and metal form a continuous, level surface. Begin laying the new brick courses at once.

4 Laying the new brick. Starting at one end of the new lintel, spread the top and ends of the first brick with mortar; slide the brick into the opening. Spread the top and the inner end of a second brick with mortar, and lay it beside the first brick. Then spread mortar on the two ends of a third brick and set it on top of the first two, centered over the joint between them. Repeat this three-brick pattern at the other end of the opening. Then fill in all the bricks across the lower course, and lay a second course over them.

For a finished appearance, smooth all the new mortar with a jointer so that it will match the original wall, and use a tuck pointer to push mortar into the space between the top of the second course and the bottom of the old lintel.

Replacing Crumbling Mortar in Firebrick Joints

Repairing crumbling mortar joints. To reset loose firebricks with new fireplace mortar, first chip away as much of the old mortar as possible with a cold chisel, and brush away any soot and other debris with a wire brush. Then wash down the joints and the area around them with a wet rag, to provide a damp base for the new mortar. Using a caulking gun loaded with a tube of fireplace mortar, fill the opened joints *(top left)*. With a putty knife, smooth the mortar flush with the surrounding firebricks *(bottom left)*, as you scrape excess mortar from their faces.

Let the mortar cure for 24 hours before you light a fire. The first fire will darken the fresh mortar to match the color of the existing mortar.

The Work at the Top: How to Improve a Chimney

The most efficient chimney is one that carries smoke upward and—with the exception of a yearly visit from Saint Nick—allows a minimum of foreign matter to descend. But various things can happen to interfere with this ideal state of affairs. Masonry can crumble with age. A new building nearby can play hob with the draft. Over the summer, when the fireplace is not in use, the debris of summer storms and of nesting birds, squirrels or raccoons can clog the flue or come to rest on the smoke shelf.

To check for such problems, an annual inspection is in order. Before you light the first fire of autumn, open the damper and shine a strong flashlight up the flue. If you see any obstructions, give the chimney a thorough cleaning (pages 120-122)—a measure that will simultaneously remove soot and creosote deposits. Then add a wire-mesh screen, a chimney cap or a chimney-top damper to help keep the chimney clear in the future.

A more serious problem is a fireplace that lets smoke back into the house, a sign that the chimney is not drawing properly. This may be caused by a chimney crown that is not beveled sharply enough to direct air currents upward, over the flue. Or the chimney may not be tall enough. To draw properly, a chimney should extend at least 3 feet above the point where it passes through the roof. It should also be 2 feet higher than the highest point of such protrusions as dormers or any building within 10 feet. Even a tree that has grown tall can affect the draft of a chimney that was previously trouble-free.

It is relatively easy to reshape a flawed chimney crown—or to construct a new one—with concrete made with portland cement, available at brickyards or from building-materials suppliers. A chimney cap, which can add as much as 2½ feet to a chimney, may supply the needed height, as well as deflecting cross winds that cause downdrafts in a flue. If more height is necessary, you can extend a chimney with terra-cotta flue liner. Before you begin work on this extension, have a sheet-metal fabricator make a metal sleeve of the desired height; slip the sleeve over the existing flue, anchoring it temporarily with silicone caulk.

If the added height stops the smoking problem, replace the sheet-metal sleeve with a permanent liner made of terra-cotta tile. The liner comes in 2-foot lengths and can be cut with a power saw equipped with a masonry-cutting blade. To install the liner, first remove the existing crown or any decorative brickwork at the chimney top. Then build up the flue and the chimney extension (opposite).

Leaking smoke anywhere along the length of the chimney is the most serious problem of all—it means there are cracks in the masonry that pose a fire hazard. If you suspect a leaking chimney, perform this simple test. Cover the top of the chimney with an old towel. Then place a smoke bomb or a smoky flare on the smoke shelf and close the damper; such bombs and flares are available at stores that specialize in equipment for wood stoves and fireplaces. Examine the exterior of the chimney—from outdoors, on each floor, and in the attic—for smoke. If the chimney leaks, do not use the fireplace until the problem is fixed.

A leaking chimney is often an old one, predating the use of flue liners, and can be fixed by installing a stainless-steel flue liner (pages 23-25). If the chimney has a terra-cotta flue liner, however, the leak is probably caused by deteriorating mortar joints in the liner. Such a flue must be repaired—a job that may involve tearing down the outer wall of the chimney, and one that is best left to a professional.

Extending the Flue to Improve the Draft

1 Removing the old crown. Wearing gloves and safety goggles to protect yourself from flying chips, use a ball-peen hammer and a masonry chisel to break away the crown of concrete or mortar around the flue. Work from the flue liner toward the outer walls of the chimney, to prevent chips from falling down the flue. Collect and save as much of the rubble as possible; you can use it as filler later, when you are rebuilding the crown.

2 **Installing the flue extension.** Spread fireplace mortar on the top edge of the old flue liner, then position the terra-cotta liner extension on top of it. Build up the walls of the chimney *(pages 72-73)* and add more liner sections, if necessary, ending the brick walls 8 inches below where you want the top of the flue to be. Mix the chips saved from the old crown with some leftover mortar, and wedge them between the flue extension and the last course of brick.

3 **Making a new crown.** Frame the top of the chimney extension with 2-by-4s, and pour concrete made with portland cement into the frame to form the new crown. Construct the 2-by-4 frame to fit snugly around the chimney top, lapping two opposite sides of the frame over the other two sides and extending the frame 1 inch above the final row of bricks. Moisten the bricks, then pour concrete into the frame to just above the top of the frame *(below, center)*.

As the concrete begins to stiffen, use a mason's trowel to slope the concrete surfaces up toward the flue liner on all four sides, leaving at least 4 inches of the liner exposed above the concrete *(below)*. Mist the concrete with a garden hose every few hours to keep it damp for four days. When the concrete is cured, remove the frame of 2-by-4s; to do this, simply tap the overlapping board ends with a hammer until the frame comes apart.

Keeping Animals Out and Hazardous Cinders In

Making a wire-mesh screen. With a piece of chalk, mark the inside dimensions of the flue on the center of a 36-inch square of ½-inch hardware cloth, then extend the four sides of the rectangle to the edges of the cloth and cut away the corners with tin snips. Fold the mesh flaps along the sides of the rectangle to form an open-ended box. Spread fireproof silicone caulk along the open end of the box, then push the box down into the flue until the mesh cap extends 6 inches above the flue top *(inset)*.

Two Kinds of Caps to Cover a Chimney Top

Easy-to-install prefabricated caps. The semi-enclosed terra-cotta cap *(near right)*, also called a chimney pot, is mortared to the top of the existing flue. It can solve a downdraft problem by extending the flue and deflecting winds, but it may be a hindrance to chimney cleaning. Terra-cotta caps come in many shapes and sizes; be sure to choose one tall enough to extend the flue 2 feet above any tree or building within 10 feet. The combined area of the top openings should equal the area of the original flue opening. Position the cap so that the closed sides block the path of prevailing winds. The metal cap with mesh sides *(far right)* has a flange that fits down into the existing flue; other types have adjustable collars that wrap around the outside of the flue. Metal caps are available in a wide range of shapes, and they will serve to keep rain and animals out of the flue.

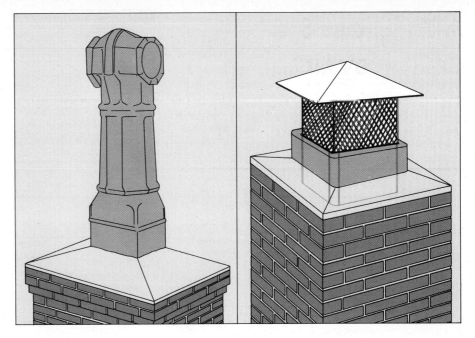

Installing a Damper at the Top of a Chimney

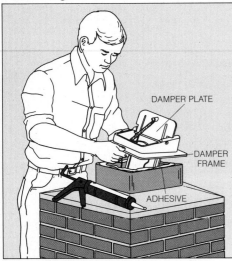

DAMPER PLATE

DAMPER FRAME

ADHESIVE

1 **Securing the damper frame to the flue.** Apply two parallel beads of adhesive, provided by the damper manufacturer, around the top edges of the flue; then press the damper frame firmly against the flue. With the damper open, drop the wire cable down through the flue into the firebox. Shake the cable vigorously a few times to release any kinks or coils.

WIRE CABLE

SETSCREW

CABLE BRACKET

2 **Installing the cable bracket.** At a point on a side wall of the firebox approximately 2 feet from the floor and midway between the front opening and the back wall, clear a slot in a horizontal mortar joint 2 inches deep and the width of the cable bracket. To make the slot, drill several holes in the joint with a masonry bit, and chip out remaining mortar with a masonry chisel. Tap the bracket into the slot with a ball-peen hammer, then run a bead of fireplace mortar between the bracket and the firebox wall to hold the bracket in place.

Pull the chain through the hole in the bracket; thread the cable through the setscrew assembly on the chain *(inset)*. Pull the cable to close the damper, then tighten the setscrew and cut the cable 1 inch below the screw.

A Stainless-Steel Chimney Lining

You can stop smoke leaks from the masonry joints of an unlined chimney by adding a stainless-steel liner. The flue must be straight from the smoke chamber to the chimney top, and large enough for a liner matched to the fireplace opening *(page 70)*.

To begin the job, take preliminary measurements. Lower a steel-tape rule down through the flue until the end of the tape is level with the juncture of smoke chamber and flue—have a helper peer up through the damper opening with a flashlight to monitor this action.

To this measurement add 8 inches for the liner extension above the chimney, plus at least 3 additional inches for every 3 feet of length to allow for liner joints. The final figure is the total length of steel pipe you will need.

Next, measure the size of the chimney opening. If the opening is a rectangle, the diameter of the flue pipe should be 1 inch less than the shorter dimension—unless a smaller flue would increase the efficiency of the fireplace *(page 70)*.

From a sheet-metal fabricator, order 24-gauge stainless-steel pipe in 3-foot lengths, crimped for 3 inches at one end of each piece so that the parts can be easily joined. Buy enough self-tapping screws to put four at each planned joint. And get a sheet of 24-gauge stainless steel at least 4 inches wider and longer than the flue opening—it will be used to make the collar on which the bottom of the finished liner will rest.

Once the metal liner is installed, you must fill the space between the pipe and the chimney walls with a special insulating mixture of portland cement, sand and perlite treated with silicone; all three are available at masonry dealers. To 2 cubic feet of portland cement—enough for a 12-by-12-inch flue on a two-story house—add 6 cubic feet of sand; then to one part of this mixture, add five parts of silicone-treated perlite. Place this mixture in a mortar-mixing box and use a hoe to combine the ingredients, then add enough water to dampen the mixture throughout without making it runny. Use a bucket and a sturdy rope to haul the insulating mixture up to the roof.

1 **Making an access hole in the chimney.** On the outside wall of the chimney, locate the point where the top of the smoke chamber meets the chimney. Remove one course of bricks above that point to start an access hole into the chimney. Make the hole at least two bricks high and as wide as the internal measurement of the chimney—usually three bricks wide is enough. Loosen the bricks by drilling through the mortar around them. Remove the bricks carefully; set them aside to be used in refilling the hole. Chip and brush away any debris to clear the passageway into the flue *(inset)*.

2 **Marking and cutting the flue collar.** Measure the inside dimensions of the flue at the chimney top, and draw a matching rectangle on a sheet of 24-gauge stainless steel. Draw a second rectangle, 2 inches longer and wider on each side, around the first. At the center of the two rectangles, draw a circle with the same diameter as the metal flue pipe; then center a second circle, 2 inches smaller, inside the first. Use tin snips to cut around the outside rectangle. At each corner, cut a slit in to the edge of the inner rectangle, positioning the four slits parallel to one another. Finally, cut out the inner circle.

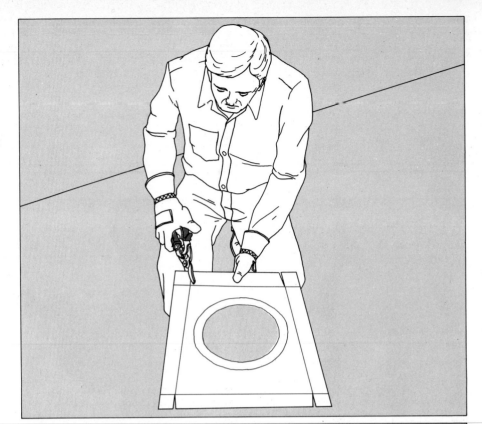

3 **Cutting tabs for the flue pipe.** Use tin snips to make radial cuts at 1-inch intervals around the edge of the inner circle of the flue collar, extending each cut to the outline of the outer circle. Bend up the resulting tabs at a 90° angle, and test them for fit against the pipe. Then bend up the edges of the rectangle in the same direction; lap the ends, forming a 2-inch flange around the outside of the collar *(inset)*.

Slide the collar, its flanges and tabs pointing upward, into the access hole in the outside wall of the chimney. The flanges should fit snugly against the walls of the chimney; rebend them if necessary to adjust the collar size. Then slide the collar down into the chimney until the top edge of the flange is flush with the bricks that form the bottom of the access hole.

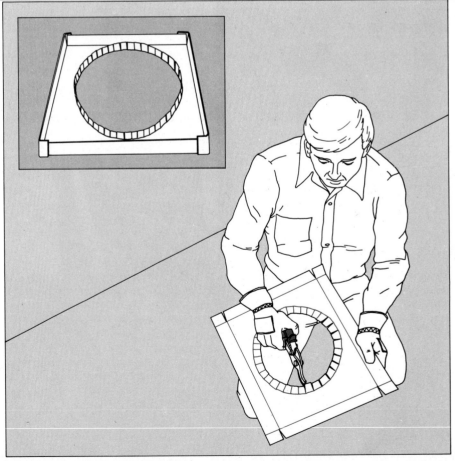

4 Anchoring the collar in place. Drill a ¼-inch hole through the flange at the front and at the back of each side; make sure that you dent the bricks beneath the flange. Do not drill into the inner chimney wall, which abuts combustible framing members. Take the collar away, and drill a ½-inch hole 1 inch deep at each point where a dent marks the bricks. Insert ½-inch heatproof steel anchors into these holes. Reposition the collar, then fasten the flange to the bricks with ¼-inch bolts. Caulk any gaps that may remain between the flue collar and the chimney walls, using special fireplace mortar.

5 Installing the flue pipe. Working on the roof with a helper, assemble the metal flue pipe a section at a time and lower it down the chimney until it meets the collar. Join adjacent sections of flue pipe with four self-tapping metal screws. Have a second helper, at the access hole, apply special fireplace mortar inside the bottom end of the pipe and slip the pipe over the tabs on the collar. At the top, leave 8 inches of pipe protruding above the chimney.

Fill the access hole with the original bricks *(page 23, Step 1)*, mortaring them in place *(page 19)*.

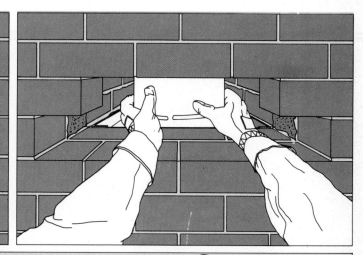

6 Insulating the flue pipe. To insulate the new stainless-steel flue, pour buckets of the perlite mixture *(page 23)* down into the space between the pipe and the chimney walls until the chimney is filled to the top. Have a helper fill the bucket on the ground, then haul each load up to the roof with a rope.

Make a chimney cap from a piece of metal flashing 1 inch longer and wider than the original flue opening, then cut a hole in the cap the size of the flue pipe. Run a bead of silicone caulk along the inner edge of the chimney, slip the cap over the flue pipe and press it down along the edges to anchor it to the brick. Caulk where the cap meets the flue pipe.

Restoring a Secondhand Stove to Active Life

A turn-of-the-century potbellied stove or an old parlor stove, complete with nickel-plated footrails and mica doors, can be a charming conversation piece in any home. But before you fire up such an antique—or even a used stove of more recent vintage—inspect it, top to bottom, and if necessary restore it to safe working order.

Most often, the repairs will be simple. An antique may need nothing more than a fresh coat of stove blacking or a new mica pane for the windows. On more recent models, the only element in need of replacement may be the gasket that keeps the firebox airtight. Even more serious flaws, such as separating seams in the body of a cast-iron stove, can usually be quickly mended with furnace cement. All of these materials are readily available at stores that sell wood stoves.

If you have acquired the stove along with a house, the place to begin your inspection is with the installation. Measure the clearances between the stove and the surrounding walls; be sure they comply with local codes (page 48). Remove the stovepipe fittings, if necessary, to inspect the pipe's passage through the ceiling or wall; the pipe should be specially insulated at these points, and the necessary clearances observed (page 48). Check the hearth for size (page 50), and replace any loose or worn sections.

Next inspect the stove itself. First determine whether it is made of cast iron or sheet metal. A cast-iron stove has the same rough texture as the outer surfaces of a cast-iron skillet; a sheet-metal stove has a smooth and often shiny surface. If the stove is sheet metal, be particularly critical. Sheet metal has a tendency to warp badly with heavy use, and an old sheet-metal stove will often not be worth the trouble of refurbishing.

Next, starting at the bottom of the stove, check the legs for cracks or missing bolts. Replace any missing bolts; if a leg is cracked, take it to a foundry for welding. In general, be sure that the legs provide stable support and that the stove sits firmly on its base.

Moving up from the legs, use a light to inspect the body of the stove for breaks in the casting (opposite). Slight separations at the seams of cast-iron stoves are commonplace and can be patched with a specially compounded furnace cement. A crack in the body, however, is more serious. If it is only a hairline crack, it can be repaired with the cement; but check the repair from time to time to be sure that the crack gets no larger. If a crack is already severe, an entire new section will have to be fabricated—a relatively expensive proposition.

Also inspect the innards of the stove. If a firebrick lining has deteriorated, chisel out the mortar between the old bricks and install new ones. If the stove has an inner lining of metal, make sure that each panel of the lining is intact. Such panels—called burn plates—may have burned through, particularly if the stove was used for coal fires. Replacement burn plates can be fabricated, but this too may be expensive. An alternative is to remove all of the plates and install a lining of firebricks.

Finally, check all of the stove's movable parts—its baffle, door handles and draft controls. A removable baffle usually rests on extensions welded to the side and back walls of the stove interior; it can be lifted up and slipped out of the stove. A door handle must keep the door shut tightly; if the catch mechanism is obstructed by soot or creosote, it may stick. So too may a damper whose plate or spindle has warped.

When you are repairing a stove, obtaining replacement parts may be a problem—unless the company that manufactured the stove still exists. If not, you will need to jury-rig the part or have the piece custom-made. But remember, if you are installing substitute parts, that it is almost impossible to drill through cast iron without chipping it. Do not try to enlarge existing holes to fit available bolts; instead, buy new bolts that are exactly the size you need.

Sealing Cracks in a Leaking Firebox

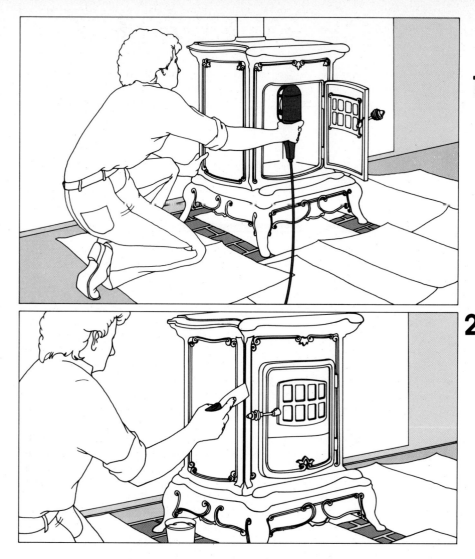

1 **Locating the cracks.** Working on a protective layer of newspaper, remove any grates, baffles or movable linings from the stove's interior, then place a trouble light or a flashlight in the empty cavity. Close the door (with a trouble light, you will have to leave the door slightly ajar for the electric cord); then darken the room and examine the outside surfaces for any sign of leaking light. Pay particular attention to the seams of the stove, where the cast-iron sections are joined. Disconnect the stovepipe, and then have a helper tilt the stove while you are inspecting the bottom.

To check for hairline cracks too fine to leak light, rub chalk lightly over the stove surface; the chalk will fill any crack, leaving a visible line. Or light a small fire and watch for wisps of smoke.

2 **Caulking an open seam.** To prepare the metal surface for the furnace cement, wire-brush the area along the open seam both inside and outside the stove, removing any loose dirt or rust; then protect the outside surface from excess cement by outlining the seam with masking tape. Working first on the inside, then on the outside, dampen the seam area with a wet cloth or sponge, and force cement into the seam with a putty knife. Remove the tape and let the cement dry for 24 hours. The first time you use the stove after this repair, keep a small kindling fire going for an hour or two, to check the tightness of the seal, before stoking the fire.

Refurbishing to Correct Minor Flaws

Polishing a worn stove. Scrub down the stove exterior with a wire brush to remove encrusted dirt and surface rust; then rub a light coat of stove blacking over the cast iron with a soft cloth. When the blacking has dried, buff the metal with a shoe brush. Polish any nickel-plated parts with ordinary metal polish.

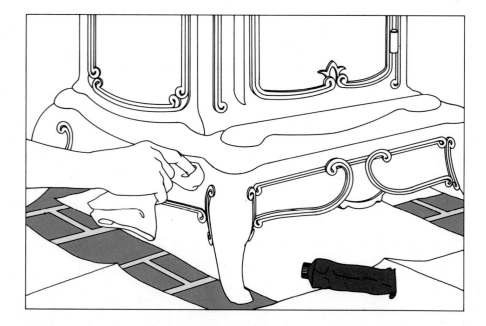

Lining an unlined stove. To insulate the bottom of a stove firebox, lay rows of firebricks on the firebox floor, beginning at the back and working forward. Plan the brick arrangement with a dry run, spacing the bricks ⅛ inch apart. Cover the bottom as completely as possible, cutting bricks as needed to fill the rows, but do not try to fill small, odd-shaped spaces at the edge of the firebox. (If the firebox floor is circular, as on a potbellied stove, you may prefer to use refractory cement, as described on page 67.)

When the dry run is complete, lift out the bricks in sequence and lay them again, this time spreading a thin coating of furnace cement on each brick surface that adjoins another brick. Do not cement the bricks to the metal floor or walls of the stove; the unequal rates of expansion of metal and brick will break the bond. Allow the cement to dry for 24 hours or more before you build a fire in the stove again.

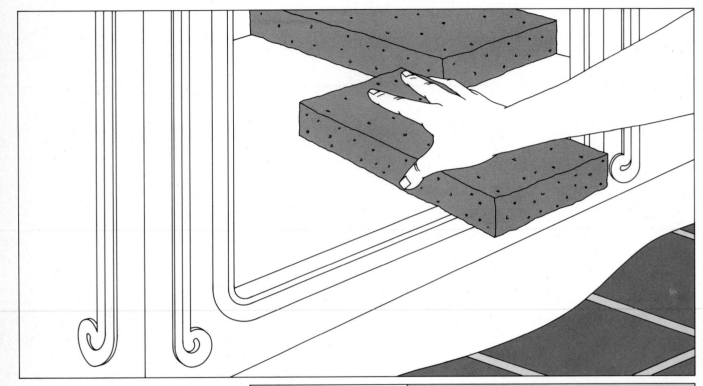

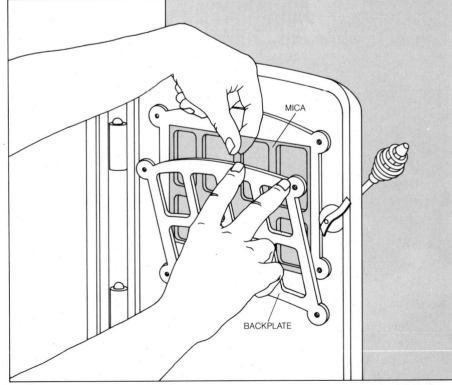

MICA

BACKPLATE

Replacing a broken stove window. Remove the screws that hold the iron plate over the back of the stove window, and slip out the broken pane. Cover the opening with a new sheet of mica (sometimes called isinglass), and trace the outline of the window opening onto the mica with a washable-ink felt-tipped marking pen. Trim the mica with scissors, leaving a margin of about ¼ inch beyond the outline. Then remove the outline with a damp cloth. Center the mica over the window while you fasten the back plate down over it, sealing the opening.

Replacing a warped damper. To remove an old stovepipe damper, disassemble the section of stovepipe containing the damper and reach inside with one hand, grasping the edge of the damper plate. With the other hand, force the damper handle inward, compressing its spring and twisting it until the spindle hump is disengaged from the flange on the plate. Pull out the spindle and remove the plate.

To install a new damper, insert the spindle through one hole into the stovepipe until the hump rests against the outside of the pipe. Then angle the spindle toward the end of the pipe, and slide the new damper plate in. Thread the spindle through the openings on the plate; then twist the spindle until the hump slides into the stovepipe. Compressing the spring on the damper handle, push the spindle through the hole on

the other side of the pipe until the spindle hump hits the first flange of the damper plate.

To add a damper to a stovepipe that never had one, drill a ¼-inch hole on one side of the pipe at least 6 inches from one end. Insert the spindle, and line it up across the width of the pipe. Press it against the far side until it leaves a mark. Drill a hole there, and insert the damper.

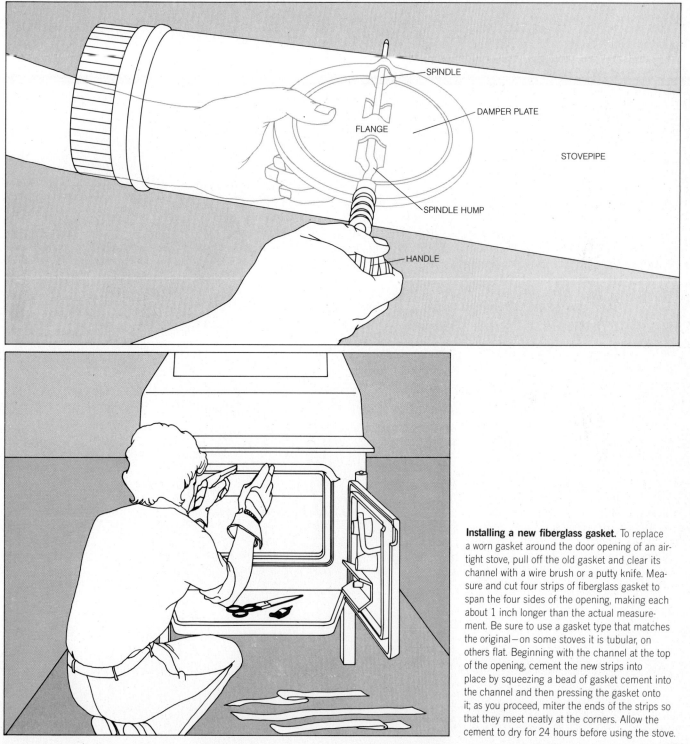

SPINDLE

DAMPER PLATE

FLANGE

STOVEPIPE

SPINDLE HUMP

HANDLE

Installing a new fiberglass gasket. To replace a worn gasket around the door opening of an airtight stove, pull off the old gasket and clear its channel with a wire brush or a putty knife. Measure and cut four strips of fiberglass gasket to span the four sides of the opening, making each about 1 inch longer than the actual measurement. Be sure to use a gasket type that matches the original—on some stoves it is tubular, on others flat. Beginning with the channel at the top of the opening, cement the new strips into place by squeezing a bead of gasket cement into the channel and then pressing the gasket onto it; as you proceed, miter the ends of the strips so that they meet neatly at the corners. Allow the cement to dry for 24 hours before using the stove.

Getting More from a Wood Stove

A number of optional accessories are available to make wood stoves more efficient or practical. Two of the best are a heat extractor, which salvages heat otherwise lost up the flue, and a stovepipe oven *(opposite, bottom)*, which adapts the stove for baking. Both are used most safely if the stovepipe temperature is monitored with a stack thermometer, still another optional accessory.

The most common kind of heat extractor consists of a metal box, with two short stovepipe connections, that is designed to replace a standard 24-inch section of stovepipe close to the firebox. The metal box has between 10 and 14 collector tubes running through it horizontally. Flue gases flowing through the box and around the tubes make them very hot. When they reach a temperature of 150° F., room air is blown through them by a small electric fan activated by a thermostat.

Most older stoves and, indeed, many newer designs can benefit from such an addition. The average stove can send intense heat—between 800° and 1,200°—into the collar of the flue, just above the firebox. If you harness some of this heat, the stove's thermal output can be boosted as much as 20 per cent. One notable exception is the airtight stove, which is designed to control the heat it generates within the firebox, so that relatively little needs to escape up the flue. An airtight stove sometimes registers only 300° to 500° at the collar.

Along with its benefits, a heat extractor raises a question of safety. In pulling heat from flue gases near the base of the flue, the extractor lowers the temperature in the rest of the stovepipe—and a cooler stovepipe increases the danger of creosote build-up, a fire hazard. If you install such a unit, the stovepipe should be cleaned twice as often as normally *(page 120)*. The tubes in the extractor box should also be cleaned. Most models incorporate a cleaning mechanism—usually a movable plate that scrapes the outside of the tubes. The cleaning mechanism should be used several times during the course of a fire.

As a further precaution when you are using a heat extractor, monitor the temperature within the stovepipe by means of a stack thermometer. This simple instrument, intended for installation on ordinary single-walled pipe, is accurate within 5 per cent and registers temperatures between 50° and 900°. A temperature just above 300° is safe; below that, creosote tends to accumulate rapidly. The thermometer is magnetic, but as a safety precaution it should also be attached to the pipe with wire.

For structural reasons, a heat extractor must rest on 24-gauge stovepipe. To avoid any interference with the draft of the stove, the unit ought to be installed a minimum of 12 inches above the firebox and, for the same reason, the stovepipe damper has to be situated between the heat extractor and the firebox. Be sure to plug the heat extractor into an electrical outlet that is not connected to a wall switch, so that you do not inadvertently turn off the fan—if the fan is turned off, the unit's heat output will be lowered and the pipes inside may overheat.

Capturing Extra Heat Directly from the Flue

1 **Inserting a heat extractor.** Take off the first two 24-inch sections of stovepipe above the stove top. Slip a 12-inch pipe section equipped with a damper *(page 29)* onto the flue collar. Slide the bottom connector pipe of the heat extractor onto the extension, orienting the extractor box so that the exposed tubes face outward, into the room. Then add a second 12-inch pipe extension to the top connector pipe and reattach the existing pipe.

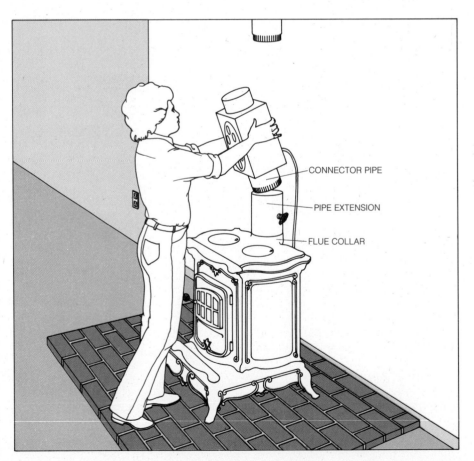

CONNECTOR PIPE

PIPE EXTENSION

FLUE COLLAR

2 **Fastening the pipes together.** Using the existing holes in the top pipe extension as guides, drill ³⁄₁₆-inch holes in the extractor's top connector pipe. Drill holes through the bottom connector pipe, using the holes in the bottom pipe extension as guides. Tighten ³⁄₈-inch No. 8 sheet-metal screws into all the holes, top and bottom.

Wiring a Stack Thermometer to the Flue

Wiring the thermometer on. Twist steel wire through the eye on one side of the thermometer. Place the thermometer against the stovepipe about 12 inches above the heat extractor. Draw the wire around the pipe and through the other eye. Pull the wire snug, but do not restrict the movement of the coils on the thermometer back. Wrap the wire around itself several turns.

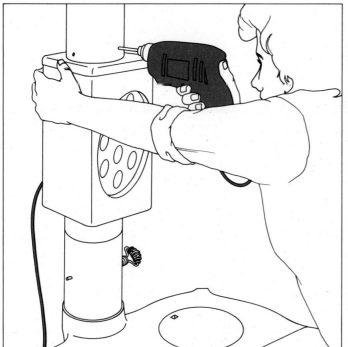

Cooking and Baking on a Wood Stove and in Its Flue

The once familiar wood-burning cookstove—with lift-out lids and warming ovens—has largely disappeared from modern kitchens. But a kettle of water can still be brought to a boil on the top of almost any wood stove, and if your stove has a cooking lid, you can lift it out and cook directly over the fire. By adding a stovepipe oven *(right)*, you can even bake with heat from the flue.

A stovepipe oven is installed as a heat extractor is, but it must be at least 24 inches above the stove top. Flue gases go through its hollow walls, heating the cylindrical baking chamber to as high as 400°. Short of regulating the intensity of the blaze inside the stove, there is no way to control the baking temperature, although the thermometer on the face of the oven door will help you to estimate the baking time.

Successful stove-top cooking with a wood fire is a matter of knowing your stove. All stove tops have hot and cool areas, but they differ with the design of the stove. Generally, the hottest section of the stove top is over the back of the firebox. If you want to cook faster, remove a lift-out lid. If you need a lower temperature, move the pan toward the front of the stove or raise it above the surface with a cast-iron trivet.

Any cooking vessel that is suitable for use over a gas or electric stove burner can be used on top of a wood-burning stove. Cast iron, because it retains heat well and distributes it evenly, is the traditional material for pans and griddles. Soapstone also has long been used for griddles. Soapstone requires no grease or cooking oils and is prized for its ability to diffuse heat uniformly.

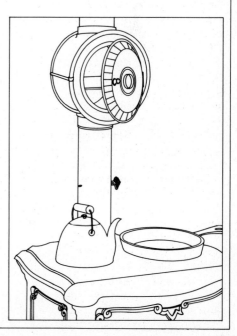

The Warm Heart of the Home

"Americans," an architect observed some years ago, "seem to regard the right to own and operate a fireplace as some kind of Constitutional guarantee. You can cut all sorts of corners in designing a house for a client and get away with scarcely a notice, but deny him his fireplace and he feels a deep sense of deprivation and loss." Just why this should be so, the architect was not sure, although he suspected that love of hearth had more to do with primordial notions of home and family than it did with staying warm.

The fact is that a fireplace, or even its psychological surrogate, the wood stove, is an island around which all sorts of domestic activities circulate. Like a good friend, it offers entertainment, comfort and security, and because it carries so much emotional freight, it can often be the supreme and overriding design element in the room.

Safety, efficiency and local building codes must, of course, always be taken into consideration—even when a fireplace or a stove is used primarily to make an esthetic statement. But within those parameters, the possibilities for personal expression are enormous.

Take, for example, the matter of location; depending on where it is placed, a heating source can elicit a wide range of responses. Put it in the center of a room and automatically chairs are drawn up around it like so many wagons circling a campfire. Tuck it in a corner and it becomes a cozy inglenook for quiet conversation. Place it in a spacious front hall, where it is found in so many Victorian mansions, and it literally radiates a warm welcome to anyone who comes in the door. At the opposite extreme, a stove or fireplace installed in a kitchen, a playroom or a master bedroom immediately turns that room into a domestic cocoon, far removed from the outside world.

The decorative possibilities of fireplaces and stoves also spring from their physical design, which can largely determine the overall character of a room. A fireplace framed in adobe or rough-dressed fieldstone, or crowned by a mantel made from a hand-hewn beam, establishes the basic theme of casual country living. Painted wood paneling and a mantel trimmed with ornamental molding suggest just as surely the formal style of Colonial times. Hand-painted tiles, carved marble pilasters, sinuous cast-iron facings—each establishes its own set of stylistic associations with other cultures and other times.

By contrast, a completely unconventional design approach—especially to a subject as tradition-steeped as a fireplace—can produce spectacular results. The high-tech, steel-encased fireplace and chimney on page 35 show the decorative impact of this kind of freethinking, as does the irreverent assembly of concrete conduits on page 40.

The decorative possibilities of a wood stove are equally varied. Plebeian potbellies, florid parlor stoves, sleek Scandinavian hot boxes—each sets a particular decorative theme for a room. Even the stovepipe has design potential. Customarily treated as an anonymous necessity and painted a disappearing mat black, it can be played up for all it is worth. One showy possibility is stainless-steel stovepipe; another is stovepipe painted in one or more of the heat-resistant paints that are used to color-code pipe in industrial plants. For a handsome example of this approach, see opposite.

Finally, there are the decorative benefits gained by imposing a secondary function on the heating source. On the following pages are examples of how intrepid designers have used a chimney as a room divider, a support for built-in seating, a control tower for various internal climate-regulating devices, a display device for plants and unusual artifacts, even a solar-heat storage sink.

Solar back-up. In this integrated heating system, a massive stone fireplace is handmaiden to a solar collector on the roof. The huge tank at the rear stores 2,000 gallons of sun-heated water; while the fireplace is being used, this water also circulates through a fire-heat exchanger, carrying back extra BTUs.

The Freestanding Hearth at Center Stage

In a large room where there is ample space to move about and much space to heat, a central stove or fireplace can provide a natural focus for the family's activities. Being the center of attention, however, places special demands on the installation's visual quality. The heat source and its stack must look good from all sides in all seasons, even in the warm months when a fireplace or a stove is technically only unused furniture.

As the three examples shown here demonstrate, the best solutions have about them the character of sculpture. The restored cast-iron parlor stove below is a Victorian extravaganza of baroque form and chrome ornament. The fireplace at top, opposite, is a sleek metal monolith in the high-tech mode. The fireplace at bottom, opposite, borrows from the earthy traditions of pottery in the softly curving lines of its terra-cotta flue and base. And all three are positioned to radiate heat in all directions.

Pillar of fire. As part of an ultramodern apartment renovation, walls have been removed and an existing fireplace flue incorporated in a new fireplace column. Finished in chrome and steel, the fireplace becomes the dominant feature of the room. A second column, foreground, contains conventional heating ducts.

Reprise for an antique. With load-bearing roof columns as its proscenium arch, a grand old parlor stove holds center stage in the living room of a new solar house. The quarry-tile floor absorbs heat from the sun as well as from the stove. Isinglass windows ring the firebox, creating semi-circles of flickering firelight.

Vulcan's hearth. In a modernized medieval château, an extraordinarily large amphora-shaped flue overhangs a fire pit to provide the communal center of the grand salon. Terra-cotta tiles, which absorb and then radiate heat, sheath both elements. Marble pillars frame the area and provide stability and support for the flue.

35

Scaled down for heat. This fireplace has been made to work better without losing face: Its firebox opening was reduced by means of a splendid copper frame.

Handsome Is as Handsome Does

With energy conservation of prime importance, the fireplace now must be more than atmospheric: It must provide maximum heat with minimum fuel. To that end, two main fireplace-design trends have evolved. The first type, in the installations opposite and at right below, is a product of modern technology. One fireplace (below, right) works on the principle of heat exchange: Cool air is drawn into a chamber around the fire and pumped out as heated air through vents above. In the other (opposite), the draft is improved by a reduction in the size of the firebox opening.

The second type, as old as the hills, is shown in two views below. It uses the principle of heat storage, in which a small firebox is enclosed in a massive baffled chimney. The heat collects, making the tile-covered chimney exterior pleasantly warm for a long period of time. The benches, or Sitzbänke, around the chimney may be the best seats in the house.

Thermal mass. A direct descendant of the mighty Kachelöfen of Central Europe, this handsome tile-faced masonry stove heats the whole house. When the stove is filled with a load of logs and fired at full blast for about an hour, its tiles absorb enough heat to radiate warmth for another twelve. Access to the firebox is through a rear wall in the hall, as shown at right.

Climate tower. Reminiscent of the designs of Frank Lloyd Wright, this highly decorative two-story chimney breast conceals a complex system for circulating warm and cool air. In winter, cool air is drawn into the double-walled fireplace and vented as warmed air through grilles in the face. Other ducts gather hot air under the roof, returning it to floor level in winter and venting it through the roof in summer.

Heating Sources That Do Double Duty

When interior space is at a premium, it sometimes makes sense to use a stove or a fireplace for more than heat. One obvious second purpose, so old that it tends to be overlooked, is cooking.

In the kitchen at right, a 1930 Glenwood range is a backup cookstove for parties as well as an extra heat source when temperatures drop below zero. Similarly, more than heat is provided by a fireplace carved into a granite outcropping (far right), which divides the grotto room and provides niches for plants. In the third example, below, the framing of a small factory-built insulated fireplace is joined to a wall of furniture, the whole more substantial than the sum of its parts. In a fourth approach to dual-duty use (page 40), a fireplace combines warmth with amusement.

Auxiliary cookstove. A venerable wood-fired range makes a handsome decorative object in the modern country kitchen, and it is hooked up and ready to go whenever additional heat or cooking facilities are needed. Its flue, the flue of the airtight stove in the background and the stainless-steel furnace flue, foreground, all pass through the master bedroom overhead to form a warming canopy above the bed.

Fireplace as modular furniture. In the beach house at left, storage cabinets and sectional seating flank a prefabricated fireplace to form a single compact unit. Completely insulated within its own metal shell, the heating element nestles safely against the walls and the woodwork; there is no need for clearance.

Subterranean room divider. A massive granite rock, retained *in situ* as the designer of the house found it, has been fitted out as the fireplace of a grottoed interior. The rock divides the two levels of the living room and the dining room, and serves as a planter for creeping vines.

Anthropomorphic hearth. Common sewer pipes form mouth, nostrils and eyes on this funny-face bedroom fireplace; the pupils in the eyes are plastic balls.

Huge Multipurpose Stoves Built of Brick or Stone

For centuries, people in the cold regions of Europe and Asia where timber was abundant heated their homes with masonry stoves—large, often two-ton, structures of brick, stone, or clay covered with tile or porcelain. Domestic life revolved around these stoves: Food was cooked in them, clothes were dried over them, sometimes they even had sleeping niches built into the top.

Designs were as diverse as the cultures in which the stoves developed—Finland, Hungary, Russia, Switzerland, Austria, Germany, Afghanistan, Korea—but the principle was the same: A fire was built in a firebrick-lined firebox and kept going for about an hour until all blue flame disappeared, indicating that all carbon monoxide gases were gone. The firebox door was then shut, and so was the blast gate—a chimney damper—if one existed.

The hot gases were trapped and made to circulate through a maze of three to six masonry flues, where heat was absorbed and eventually transferred through the masonry into the room. Although a masonry stove needed three hours to heat completely and its outside rarely got warmer than 200° F., it held heat for 12 to 24 hours.

Masonry stoves may have evolved from systems developed by the Romans and Chinese to heat the tiled floors in their baths and homes: Hot smoke from a fire under one end of the room eddied through a maze of columns, as much as 18 inches high, on which the floor was supported. Later versions of this baffled flue varied widely. The whitewashed brick stove of Russia, for example, had a firebox flanked on one side by vertical or horizontal flues (inset, right). Ovens might be built on one or both sides of the firebox, and occasionally the firebox was set chest-high to double as a bread oven; the height made it easy to remove the bread.

In Finland, the stoves often were cylindrical in shape and had a firebox door about halfway up. The flue system carried the smoke in an arching pattern, like that of a fountain, up from the firebox and down around it. The ornately decorated 8- to 11-foot-tall tile-covered stoves of Germany, Austria and Switzerland also were usually round, and the flues were also arranged so that the smoke traveled in a fountain pattern. In most homes, such a stove sat in a corner, often against the wall of a service area, with doors in that wall for loading the stove and removing ashes.

In America, immigrant groups such as the Pennsylvania Dutch and the Mennonite and Moravian communities, who clung to their traditional ways of living, built masonry stoves out of brick. Where wood was not readily obtainable, the immigrants made do with whatever fuels they found: One Mennonite group in Nebraska in the late 1800s used straw—feeding it into the firebox continuously for less than an hour; the resulting heat warmed the house for the rest of the day.

Although masonry stoves are usually considered quaint holdovers from the days before central heating, interest in them has revived since the mid-1970s, particularly in New England, where the cost of heating oil skyrocketed. To fit the stoves into existing homes, they are sometimes installed on a 1-foot concrete pad in the basement and tied into an existing chimney. The stoves generally range in height from 6 to 8 feet and can heat areas from 800 to 2,400 square feet—although in one case a brick stove 22 feet high was installed in a boys' school in New Hampshire.

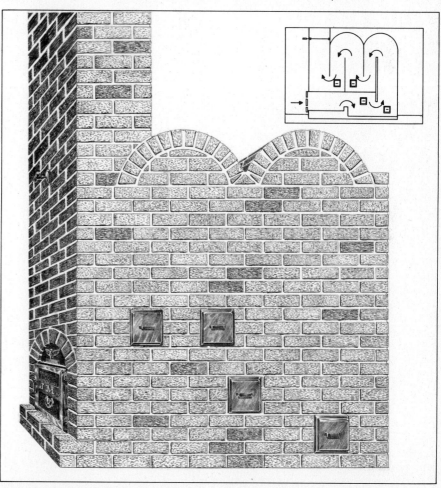

A modern brick oven. This modern adaptation of a traditional arched Russian stove is 7 feet high and has five flues separated by baffles. The firebox is lined with firebrick grouted with special fireplace mortar; its opening is covered with a metal door. A handle opens and closes a damper plate built into the last flue. Cleanout plugs are placed in each flue.

Critical link. This stainless-steel chimney T will channel the smoke from a wood stove through the framed wall opening and into a chimney pipe running up the outside of the house. The protruding snout of the T connects with a run of horizontal pipe from inside the house, and the collar around the top anchors the first vertical section of chimney pipe. Insulation within the metal walls allows the T, and the straight chimney pipe that goes with it, to be installed just 2 inches from the combustible siding.

"Fire," wrote Henry David Thoreau, "is the most tolerable third party." Whether or not you share that conviction, there is no doubt that the most energy-efficient way to welcome fire into your home is in a modern, airtight wood stove. Despite an enduring association in many minds with log cabins and country stores, the wood stove at its best is a skillfully engineered combustion chamber that produces heat from wood as efficiently as most home furnaces create heat from gas or oil.

Of course, its warming power is not the only quality that makes a fire so companionable. Even the practical Benjamin Franklin conceded that an open fire was pleasant to look at. Although he blamed the 18th Century fireplace for a dreadful assortment of ailments, from damaged eyesight to rotted teeth, he nevertheless designed his own stove without a door—so that people could watch the flames.

Some modern stove manufacturers circumvent these conflicting desires with doors that display the fire when open but keep the firebox airtight when closed. If this seems an unsatisfactory substitute for watching flames at play in a traditional fireplace, an alternative is a ready-made metal fireplace with glass doors. Freestanding models provide the charm of an open fire with a minimal investment. A heavily insulated zero-clearance version, designed to be placed against an existing wall and encased in new walls, looks like a real fireplace. Yet its insulated firebox and glass doors, plus built-in extras such as air-supply ducts and heat circulators, make it far more efficient than a masonry fireplace.

Whichever form of ready-made heater you choose, its installation should be easy. You may be able to vent your stove or factory-made fireplace into an existing flue. If not, erecting a new flue of metal chimney pipe is a job that requires only simple tools and basic carpentry techniques. Chimney pipe for stoves is made of two or three concentric cylinders, filled with air or insulating material and sealed at each end; fireplace chimney pipe is made of three concentric cylinders with unsealed ends so that air flows freely between the sections. Metal spacers and metal supports to hold the new flue in place are supplied with the pipe, and the pipe sections are designed to lock together in a jiffy.

In addition to being simple to assemble, metal chimney pipe has two other advantages. For one, it is far safer than the single-walled stovepipe traditionally used to vent those old-time potbellies. Metal flue pipe also allows a flexibility that is impossible with a masonry chimney. Sections of pipe unlock as easily as they lock together, so if you ever want to move your stove or fireplace—from room to room or house to house—the chimney can go with it.

A Number of Designs to Suit Varied Needs

The increased popularity of wood as a heating fuel has been matched by a bewildering proliferation of wood stoves on the market. You should have little trouble finding one ideally suited to your needs, however, once you know what to look for: There are a few general principles that apply to all wood stoves.

Assuming that your stove will be a major heat source, your primary concerns should be heating capacity and heating efficiency. One is a function of the stove's physical components, the other of its design—but the two are closely related. The heating capacity of a stove—its maximum heat production—is determined by three factors. These are the size of the firebox, the surface area of the stove, and the stove's thermal mass—the total weight of its heat-absorbing materials, such as metal and firebrick.

The firebox size limits the amount of fuel the stove can hold, giving you an idea of how long a load of wood can burn and how hot the fire can get. The thermal mass absorbs heat and radiates it slowly, so a stove with a large thermal mass will continue to supply heat long after the fire is out. And—since every

square inch of the stove's surface is a source of radiant heat—the larger the surface, the more heat you can count on. Because each of these factors is related to the stove's size, a large stove can usually be expected to produce more heat than a smaller one of similar design.

The heating efficiency of a stove is a measure of the stove's ability to extract heat from a given amount of wood. Heating efficiency is usually expressed as the percentage of potential energy released by the burning wood within the stove, as opposed to the energy that goes up the flue in the form of hot air and combustible but unburned gases. Modern stoves range in efficiency from 20 per cent to more than 60 per cent.

Efficiency is determined largely by precise control of the air that enters the firebox. In the least efficient stoves, air seeps in through gaps at the seams and cracks around the doors, as well as through the air-intake vents. You can regulate the intensity of the fire—but only roughly—by setting the vents to control the draft and by partially closing the flue damper to limit the flow of gases that are escaping from the firebox.

So-called airtight stoves are superbly efficient because they have sealed seams and doors machined for a close fit or fitted with fiberglass gaskets, so that air can enter the firebox only through vents especially positioned to direct air to the part of the fire where it is most needed. In addition, the flammable gases, instead of escaping up the chimney, are burned to provide more heat. The usual method of achieving this secondary combustion is to redirect the gases, via baffles, over the wood flames, a process that boosts the temperature of the gases above their ignition point, and to provide new air for this process with a second vent.

The performance of a stove will also be affected to some extent by how it is used. Under average conditions a stove performs best when it is burning at nearly maximum capacity. If it is too big for the space it is meant to heat, and must consequently be fired at a low setting, dangerous amounts of flammable creosote will build up in the flue. If it is so small that is must always be operated at peak levels, it will need constant refueling.

To estimate the stove size you need, consult the manufacturer's literature on

Modern Designs That Stress Heat Output

The basic box stove. A box stove completely encloses the fire, drawing air in through a vent located in or under the loading door. A good box stove should have a baffle above the firebox *(inset)*, which will serve to force volatile gases past the air inlet and thus allow secondary combustion before the gases enter the flue.

In its most basic form, the box stove produces only radiant heat: Increasing the surface area by embossing it with relief patterns increases the heating capacity. The most efficient box stoves are airtight; their seams are sealed with furnace cement, and their doors are machined to a close fit or sealed with a fireproof gasket. The heating efficiency of common kinds of box stoves ranges from 30 to 50 per cent.

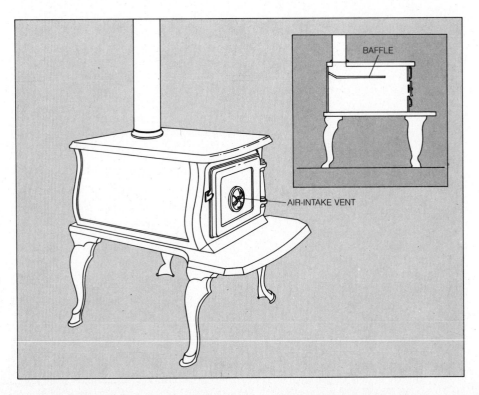

BAFFLE

AIR-INTAKE VENT

the maximum heating capacities of various models. Usually the heating capacity is expressed in the cubic feet of space a stove will heat, but it may also be given in the form of BTUs (British thermal units). A stove with a rating of 20,000 BTUs will heat an average 15-by-18-foot room. At best, however, these standards are approximate: Doors, windows, ceiling heights, insulation and even outdoor temperatures can require different BTUs for two rooms of identical volume.

Very likely, you will find exactly how efficiently a stove works in your space only after you have installed it and fired it up, although you may be able to get some helpful guidance from a neighbor who is heating a similar room with wood or from a professional who has had experience with wood heat in your area.

Performance of a stove—as well as its useful life—is affected also by the materials it is made of. Stoves may be constructed of metal sheets or plates, of cast iron, or of metal frames covered with tile or soapstone. Thin sheet metal heats and cools quickly, an advantage in situations—such as weekend cabins—where quick, short-term warmth is often needed. Cast iron and heavy metal plates warm more slowly but retain heat for hours. Tile and soapstone, noted for their

beauty, retain heat even longer than iron—and radiate it less intensely. In fact, tile never gets hot to the touch, so tile stoves are especially desirable in areas where children are likely to be.

Sheet metal, the least expensive of these stove materials, has some drawbacks. The metal may warp, causing leaks at the joints. In addition, oxidation, which takes place whenever a fire is burning, may eventually burn holes through sheet metal if it is thin. The best sheet-metal stoves have firebrick liners that reduce warping and oxidation while increasing thermal mass. Better still are stoves made of good steel boiler plate, at least ¼ inch thick, which can be expected to last as long as cast iron.

Cast iron resists warping and oxidation, but it is brittle. It may crack with extreme temperature changes (for example, if cold water is spilled on a hot stove) or when sharply struck (as by a heavy log thrown into the firebox). Cast iron is least satisfactory when thin: It is then especially subject to cracking.

How well the stove is made is another consideration. The workmanship of a cast-iron stove is most apparent at the joints, which are usually bolted together and sealed with furnace cement. Make sure that the bolts are tight and that the

cement has been evenly applied. Joints on sheet-metal or metal-plate stoves should be welded with a neat, smooth continuous bead, rather than with scattered spot welds. When looking at any stove, check for a tight fit of all parts, especially the door and its latch.

Finally, if your stove will be in constant use through a long winter, ease of operation is bound to be appreciated. The stove door should be large enough for easy loading, and you should be able to clean the stove without undue effort or mess. A stove with a grate is easier to clean than one that burns wood on the firebox floor. And a removable ashpan beneath the grate helps to make cleaning easier still.

On high-efficiency stoves, a common feature that simplifies operation is a thermostatic control of air-intake vents, but it may be a mixed blessing. Such a control, which automatically closes the vents as the fire heats up, works handsomely once the fire is burning well. But when a fire is in its earlier stages, the control operates less effectively, and can result in a loss of efficiency. For many people, however, this initial loss is more than offset by the convenience of having a stove that requires no tending after the fire is well under way.

The hollow-walled circulating stove. A circulating stove is a box stove encased by a cabinet of sheet metal. Room air, moved by convection patterns or by a fan, circulates between the firebox and the cabinet (inset), where it is warmed before being returned to the room. A thermostatic control, linked to the primary air intake, automatically regulates the air supply for the fire. Some circulating stoves have a secondary air intake above the fire to provide air for combustion of volatile gases. A firebrick liner increases the stove's thermal mass and hence its heat retention. The best circulating stoves have a heating efficiency of 60 to 70 per cent.

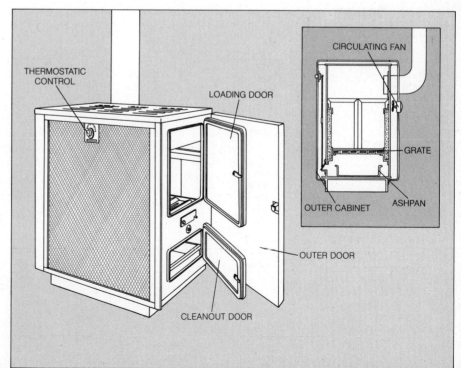

THERMOSTATIC CONTROL

LOADING DOOR

CIRCULATING FAN

GRATE

OUTER CABINET

ASHPAN

OUTER DOOR

CLEANOUT DOOR

The versatile combination stove. Because its doors can be left open or closed, a combination stove gives you a choice of looking at the fire or of enjoying the heating efficiency of an airtight box stove. Most combination stoves have a hand-operated air-intake vent, a firebrick-lined firebox, an adjustable smoke damper in the flue collar, and a removable spark screen for fire-viewing safety. With the doors closed, a combination stove burns wood with heating efficiency that ranges from 50 to 60 per cent.

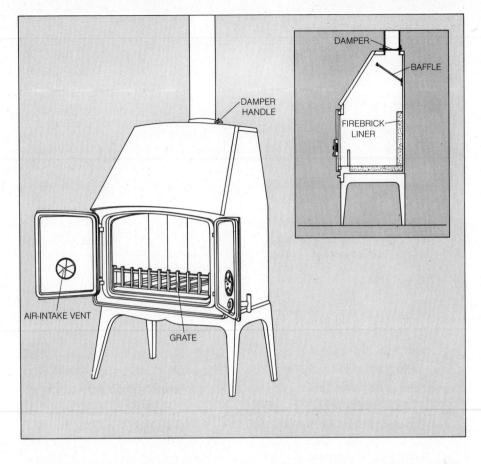

Traditional Designs with a Touch of Nostalgia

The potbellied stove. Designed to accommodate the high flames of a roaring fire, a potbellied stove is usually inexpensive and durable, and the top can be used for light cooking. Logs rest on a shakable grate, which lets ashes fall to the bottom of the stove. Air reaches the fire through a hand-operated vent in the cleanout door at the bottom. Another vent in the loading door provides air for secondary combustion of gases.

Because few potbellied stoves are made with tightly fitted parts, it is difficult to regulate the air flow with any precision. The flue damper can adjust the draft to some extent, but the maximum efficiency is only about 30 per cent.

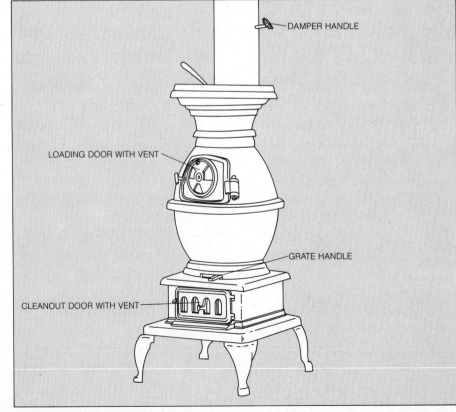

The Franklin stove. This hybrid fireplace-stove, a distant relative of a design patented by Benjamin Franklin, offers more amenity than efficiency. With the doors open, it works like a fireplace. With the doors closed, air reaches the fire through intake vents in the doors. Because air also leaks in around the doors, the burning rate must be controlled by the flue damper. The efficiency of a Franklin with doors closed is about 30 per cent.

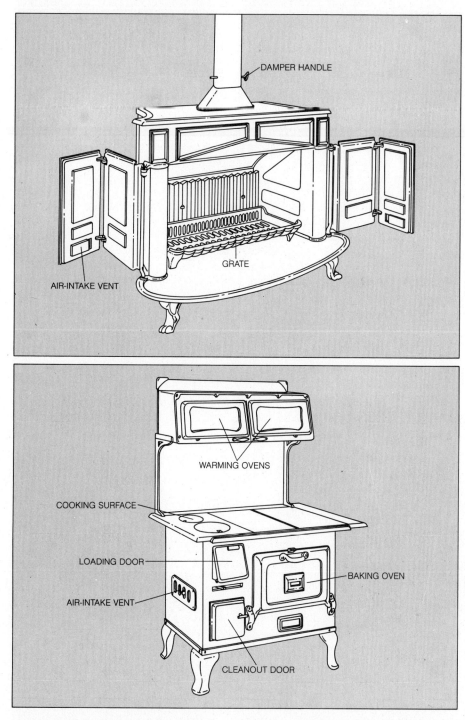

DAMPER HANDLE

AIR-INTAKE VENT

GRATE

WARMING OVENS

COOKING SURFACE

LOADING DOOR

AIR-INTAKE VENT

BAKING OVEN

CLEANOUT DOOR

The cookstove. Less convenient than modern kitchen ranges and less efficient than the more advanced heating stoves, a cookstove nevertheless both cooks and heats, an attractive combination of capabilities. The small firebox requires frequent stoking, but the large cast-iron thermal mass of the range retains and radiates heat well. The firebox heats the cooking surface directly, and hot gases from the fire are channeled around the adjacent oven to provide heat for baking; the gases then escape through a flue in the back of the stove.

Choosing an Antique with Care

An old parlor stove in an antique store or a potbellied stove at an auction may conjure up cozy images of Victorian family life or of cracker-barrel country stores. But the images may well be warmer than the reality: Most old stoves are better conversation pieces than heaters. During the heyday of wood heat, a wood stove was probably fired continually throughout the heating season. This constant use took its toll on even the best stoves.

When you are tempted to buy an old stove for heating, do not be taken in by a new coat of stove blacking. Examine the stove for flaws before you buy it *(page 26)*. If it is in good condition or can be repaired with reasonable effort and cost, evaluate it as you would a new stove for its heating capacity, efficiency and ease of operation. Chances are high that its potential performance will not measure up to that of a modern stove, but esthetic considerations will probably tip the balance. The charm of a working antique is hard to resist.

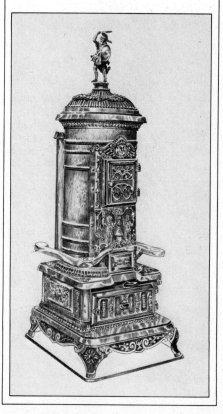

Quick but Safe Installation of a Wood Stove

Adding the warmth and character of a wood stove to an average home takes about a weekend's work. The major part of the job involves cutting passageways for the flue—the metal pipes that channel smoke and hot gases up through the house and out a hole in the roof. If your roof is covered with tile or slate, you may need to have a professional cut the roof hole, but the passageways inside the house are easy to cut and the various pipe sections and supports come in ready-to-assemble form.

Begin by choosing a location for the stove that will combine heating efficiency with safety. A wood stove heats most effectively when it is placed where its warmth can radiate into the room evenly from all sides. The safest venting system is one that travels straight up through the roof, with no bends or jogs where creosote and soot can collect (page 12), and that emerges at a point near the ridge, where sparks and hot smoke sail clear of the roof. In addition, you will need to observe the requirements of your local building code and the recommendations of the stove manufacturer in allowing for clearance between the stove and the walls or other combustible materials. As a general rule, 36 inches from an unshielded wall is considered a safe distance.

The installation shown opposite is a typical compromise between safety and efficiency. The stove is set in a corner of the room so that it will be out of the general flow of traffic; the metal heat shield behind it protects the walls from the stove's high temperatures. The flue runs straight up through the attic and the roof, exiting about 3 feet below the ridge, but is extended 2 feet above the ridge. If such a venting arrangement is impractical or impossible, you can run the flue up the outside of the house (pages 54-57) or into an existing masonry chimney (pages 60-61).

Once you have chosen a location for the stove, you are ready to buy the ma-terials you will need to install it. For the venting system you will need 24-gauge or heavier stovepipe and insulated chimney pipe. The stovepipe comes in several standard configurations—with oval or flared ends, for instance—to fit the flue collars of various kinds of stoves; elbows are available, as well as straight sections 12, 18 and 24 inches long.

The pipe sections fit one end inside the next, and they fasten together with sheet-metal screws. Buy enough pipe to reach from the base of the stove's flue collar to within 1 inch of the ceiling. If you are installing an imported stove, you will probably need an adapter to connect the stovepipe to the metric flue collar.

Building codes require that, once the pipe reaches the ceiling, you switch to insulated chimney pipe. Although the relatively thin walls of ordinary stovepipe radiate heat into the room, they can also be a fire hazard. In passing through a combustible surface such as a ceiling or a wall, ordinary stovepipe would require at least an 18-inch clearance all around, making a neat and unobtrusive opening impossible. Insulated chimney pipe, on the other hand, stays cool enough to re-quire only 2 inches of clearance. At the same time the insulation keeps the inside temperature of the pipe high enough to prevent the hot gases from cooling down too fast and depositing excess creosote on the interior walls of the pipe.

Two types of insulated chimney pipe are sold for use with wood stoves. The space between the pipe walls, which are made of two or three concentric cylinders, can be filled either with trapped air or with nonflammable insulation. Most insulated pipe is designed so that sections twist together, with locking bands to hold them tight; it comes in several lengths, from 3 to 36 inches.

Whatever type of chimney pipe you choose, it should come with all of the necessary accessories, made especially to fit it. These include chimney-support as-semblies, to provide support and safe clearance where sections of pipe pass through house framing, and flashing that slides down around the pipe to cover the opening in the roof and keep water from seeping in. The rectangular base of the flashing comes in several pitches to match the slope of the roof. To measure that slope, use a framing square or two rulers and a level to determine how many inches the roof rises per foot of horizon-tal run (page 101). Finally, above the flashing, a storm collar and a chimney cap fit snugly over the chimney pipe to keep it weathertight.

In addition to its flue, the wood stove will need a hearth and, if it is located near walls, a heat shield. Check with the building inspector for local requirements, but generally the hearth can be made of closely spaced bricks or a two-inch bed of sand or gravel, with a firm footing for each stove leg, laid over a piece of sheet metal. You can also buy prefabricated in-sulating hearths.

The heat shield that protects the walls near the stove is made of sheet metal—generally 28-gauge. But again, check with the building inspector for local regula-tions governing both the material to be used and the area of wall that must be covered. To install the shield, you will need a supply of 1-inch circular ceramic spacers with holes in the center, available at hardware stores. These are used to off-set the shield from the wall so that cool-ing air can circulate behind the sheet metal. If you want to paint the shield, use heat-resistant paint, also available at hardware stores.

A flue that passes through a second-story living space or a finished attic may also be required by code to be enclosed in a chase—a small stud-wall structure that surrounds the pipe and protects it from casual bumps that might unseat the locking connection between sec-tions. A model for this kind of structure is shown on page 53.

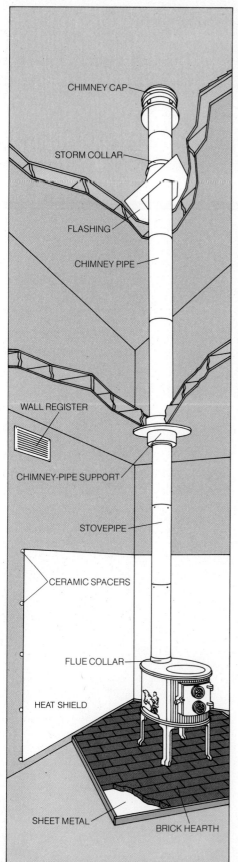

CHIMNEY CAP

STORM COLLAR

FLASHING

CHIMNEY PIPE

WALL REGISTER

CHIMNEY-PIPE SUPPORT

STOVEPIPE

CERAMIC SPACERS

FLUE COLLAR

HEAT SHIELD

SHEET METAL

BRICK HEARTH

Anatomy of an efficient stove system. The heart of this heating system is an airtight wood stove, which sits in a corner of the room so that it can radiate heat across a wide space while remaining relatively out of the way. This stove rests on a brick hearth that, in turn, is set on a protective layer of sheet metal. A metal heat shield behind the stove protects the surrounding walls; ceramic spacers between the shield and the wall allow air to circulate behind the shield, cooling any combustible wall or wall covering in back of it. A wall register installed near the ceiling distributes air heated by the stove, to help warm an adjacent room.

The stove's venting system for smoke and gases begins at the flue collar on the top of the stove; from here, these products of combustion are channeled up an uninsulated stovepipe to the insulated chimney pipe. The stovepipe and chimney pipe meet inside a chimney-pipe support that is nailed into a specially framed opening in the ceiling. From this point the chimney pipe runs straight up through a second-story room (in this example an attic), and then through openings in the ceiling and roof to the outside. There, flashing atop the roof braces the chimney pipe and, with the storm collar above it, keeps the opening weathertight. A chimney cap keeps out rain and debris, and limits downdrafts.

Preliminaries: Location, Heat Shield, Hearth

1 Positioning the stove. Place the stove temporarily in the desired position—making sure to allow for the required clearances (opposite)—and drop a plumb bob from the ceiling to the center of the flue opening. Mark the ceiling at the top of the plumb line, and drill a ¼-inch hole at that mark. Use a stiff wire to probe for the nearest joists (inset). When you touch wood, determine the distance between the hole and the joist by placing a finger against the wire where it enters the hole. Transfer this measurement to the ceiling, to mark one joist position. Then find the adjacent joist by measuring 16 inches from the first mark. Verify the joist positions by drilling tiny holes. At the midpoint between the two joists, establish a new center point for the flue opening; then use the plumb bob to adjust the stove so that it conforms to the new center point, making sure to retain the required clearances.

With the new center point for reference, use a ruler to outline a ceiling opening between joists that fits the framing measurements provided with the chimney-pipe support. Then mark the stove position on the floor with a chalk line around each leg. Remove the stove from the work area.

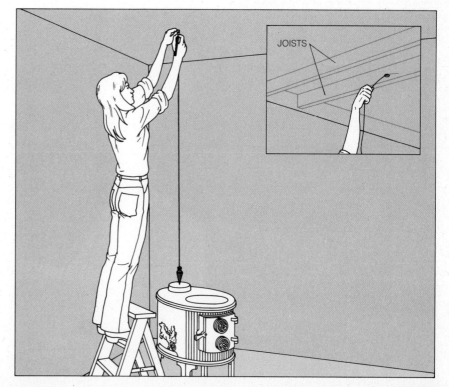

JOISTS

2 Installing a heat shield. Have a heat shield cut from 28-gauge sheet metal, and nail it to the wall studs; back the shield at each nail position with a 1-inch ceramic spacer. Have the shield cut large enough to cover any wall surface within 36 inches of the stove and within 18 inches of the stovepipe—but plan the dimensions so that no edge extends more than two inches beyond a backing stud. To locate the studs, first use a wire probe as in Step 1, then mark off the bottom of the wall at 16-inch intervals.

To mount the shield, first hold each section in place against the wall and transfer the stud locations onto it. Draw lines down the back of the shield at each stud location and, using an electric drill fitted with a 5/32-inch metal-cutting bit, drill holes through the metal at 16-inch intervals along each line. Begin and end with spacers 1 inch from the top and from the bottom. At each hole, use contact cement to fasten a ceramic spacer to the back of the shield, aligning the spacer hole with the shield hole. Remove the baseboard, if one exists, from the area to be shielded. Rest each section of shield on a piece of scrap lumber that lifts the shield 1 inch above the planned height of the hearth. While a helper steadies the shield in that position, drive tenpenny (3-inch) nails through the holes into the studs. If two shield sections meet at a corner, as in this example, make sure the edges touch.

STUD MARKS

TEMPORARY SUPPORT

3 Building a brick hearth. As a base for the bricks, cover the floor with a piece of 24-gauge sheet metal and surround it with a frame of 1-by-2 lumber; take careful measurements so that you can relocate the stove in precisely its planned position. Plan the dimensions of the metal base so that its width and length are multiples of the width and length of the bricks being used. In general, the hearth should extend 18 inches beyond the stove on all sides, unless the stove is less than 18 inches from a wall. Outline the hearth base on the floor and cut 1-by-2s to fit the outline, butt-nailing them at the corners and beveling the ends to fit flush against the walls if the frame fits into a corner, as here; toenail the ends to the wall.

Cut the sheet-metal floor covering with tin snips, and lay it inside the frame. Lay rows of unmortared bricks end to end on top of the metal, staggering the joints from row to row by starting every other row with a half brick, cut with a brickset and a small sledge *(page 74)*. Make angled cuts, as necessary, to fit the last few rows of bricks into irregularly shaped corners.

An Interior Flue That Exits through the Roof

1 **Cutting through the ceiling.** Cut away the ceiling within the outline for the chimney-pipe support *(page 49, Step 1)*. For wallboard, push the tip of a keyhole saw through and then cut. For plaster, cover the outline with masking tape and score along it with a utility knife and a straightedge. Drill ⅜-inch holes at the corners, and cut along the scored lines with a keyhole saw.

When the ceiling section has been removed, drill ⅜-inch pilot holes up through the floor above, at each corner of the opening.

2 **Cutting through the floor.** From the floor above, outline the original ceiling opening by using the four pilot holes *(Step 1)* as reference points. Enlarge the outline on the two sides perpendicular to the joists, by drawing lines parallel to and 3 inches beyond the original outline. Enlarge it on the other two sides to the joists. Drill holes at the new corners, then cut around the new outline with a saber saw.

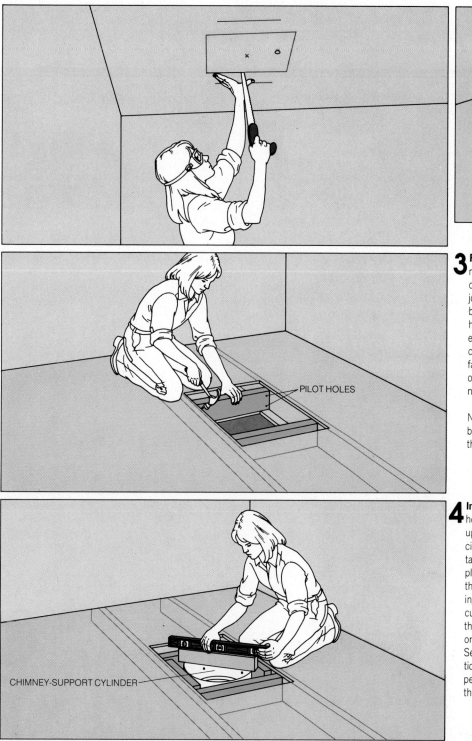

PILOT HOLES

CHIMNEY-SUPPORT CYLINDER

3 **Framing the opening.** Using lumber that matches the width and thickness of the joists, cut two braces to fit perpendicular to the joists that border the opening. As you hold each brace in position, drill two 3/32-inch pilot holes through the inside face on both ends of each brace, angling the holes into the adjacent joist. Position each brace so that its inside face is flush with the edge of the ceiling opening below, and use eightpenny (2½-inch) nails to toenail the braces to the joists.

Nail additional braces to the two joists, thus building them out until they too are flush with the sides of the ceiling opening.

4 **Inserting the chimney-pipe support.** Have a helper push the cylindrical chimney-pipe support up through the framed opening until its flat, circular collar rests against the ceiling; then tack the support cylinder temporarily in place by driving nails through predrilled holes in the cylinder, one on each side of the opening. Check the level of the cylindrical support by cutting a straight 2-by-4 slightly longer than the cylinder's diameter and resting the board, on edge, across the edges of the cylinder. Set a level atop the board, and adjust the position of the cylinder if necessary; then nail it permanently in place by driving nails through all the predrilled holes around its perimeter.

5 **Installing the stovepipe.** Measure the distance from the bottom of the cylindrical chimney-pipe support to the base of the flue collar on the stove, add 2½ inches, and assemble 2-foot lengths of stovepipe to fit this distance. Start with the bottom section, crimped end down, and slide the crimped end of the next section into the top of the first. Secure each joint as you go, using three sheet-metal screws in equally spaced holes that you predrill for them. Use an 18-inch or 12-inch length at the top end, if necessary, or trim the last section of pipe with a hacksaw for an exact fit. Then slip the top end of the completed stovepipe up into the chimney-pipe support, and push the bottom end firmly down into the flue collar.

Drill through the flanged end of the support cylinder into the stovepipe at 90-degree intervals, then screw the support cylinder and the pipe together with No. 8 sheet-metal screws.

CHIMNEY-PIPE SUPPORT

FLUE COLLAR

MARKER NAILS

6 **Cutting through the roof.** To mark the cutting lines for the hole in the roof, hang a plumb bob over each of the four inside corners of the framed floor opening, and mark the ceiling at these points. Connect the marks with a rectangular outline, and cut through the ceiling (*page 51, Step 1*). At the corners of the ceiling opening, drive tenpenny (3-inch) marker nails through the exposed roof sheathing and the asphalt shingles above it. Working on the roof, outline the rectangle formed by the marker nails and, with a hook-bladed utility knife, cut away the shingles and the roofing felt within the marked area. Then cut away the plywood sheathing beneath the roofing felt, using a saber saw or a keyhole saw.

7 **Installing the flashing.** Center the flashing over the roof opening and trace its outline on the asphalt shingles with chalk. Set the flashing aside and draw a second outline 3 inches inside the first, across the top and two thirds of the way down each side of the roof opening *(below, left)*. Cut through the shingles along this inner outline with the utility knife, and pull away the loose pieces of shingle material between the cut and the roof opening; if you encounter any roofing nails, use a pry bar to remove them.

Spread a generous layer of roofing cement on top of the shingles around the lower third of the outline you have drawn for the flashing. Then slide the flashing up under the shingle edges along the top two thirds of the outline, again removing any roofing nails that get in the way *(below, right)*. Press the lower edge of the flashing down onto the cement-coated shingles.

Lift the loose edges of the shingles around the top of the flashing, and nail the flashing to the roof

sheathing at 3-inch intervals, using roofing nails. Then nail the lower part of the sides of the flashing, but not the bottom edge, to the shingles. Cover the nailheads with dabs of roofing cement. Then, working from inside the house and starting at the chimney-pipe support, follow the manufacturer's instructions to put together the necessary sections of insulated chimney pipe to pass up through the roof opening and the flashing; the pipe should extend above the flashing a minimum of 2 inches.

FLASHING OUTLINE

FLASHING

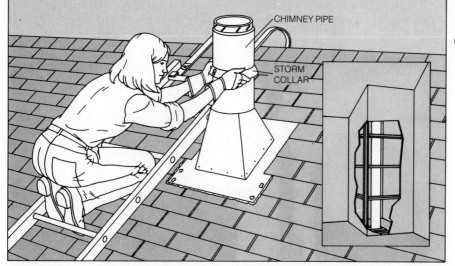

CHIMNEY PIPE

STORM COLLAR

8 **Adding a storm collar and a cap.** Slip the storm collar down over the chimney pipe until it touches the flashing. Cover the joint between the collar and the pipe with roofing cement.

Install additional sections of chimney pipe until the flue extends 3 feet above the high side of the roof where it exits, or 2 feet above any surface within a horizontal distance of 10 feet—in this case, the roof ridge. If the chimney extends more than 4 feet above the roof surface, anchor it as shown on page 57. Then slip a chimney cap into the top end of the pipe.

Inside the house, you may be required by code to build a chase—a small stud-wall enclosure—around the section of chimney pipe that runs through the second story *(inset)*.

Channeling the Heat Flow into Other Rooms

Installing a wall register. Following the manufacturer's size specifications, cut openings between two studs on both sides of the wall. Slide the halves of a two-part register into place, and fasten them to the wall with screws driven through predrilled holes in the register frame.

Install a ceiling register in a similar manner between two joists. The sleeves of a ceiling register are wider than those of a wall register, to accommodate the greater width of the joists.

Erecting a Stove Flue outside the House

Running the flue of a wood stove up the outside—rather than the inside—of a house has two advantages: It leaves more inside space clear and installation is simpler. However, an outside flue is feasible only if the roof overhang at the eaves is less than 8 inches or more than 18 inches. In addition, an outside flue results in some heat loss and risks the possibility of weak drafts and increased creosote build-up because the flue gases are cooled by outside air. Because of this cooling, an outside flue is not recommended for a building that is more than two stories high.

All the parts needed for an outside flue—pipes, spacers, fasteners and supports—are readily purchased from a stove dealer. In the house, the system uses single-walled stovepipe; outside, sections of insulated chimney pipe rise along the house wall to a safe distance above the roof. A short section of insulated chimney pipe passing through the wall joins the interior and exterior components of the system.

The initial steps in the installation of an outside flue are part of the overall planning for the entire stove installation (page 48). The most critical aspect of flue planning is the placement of the horizontal section that runs from the stove to the outside wall. This pipe should be located at least 18 inches below the ceiling and should exit from the house midway between two wall studs. In addition, the center of the wall opening should be ¼ inch higher than the center of the stovepipe elbow directly above the stove—thus creating a slight rise in the horizontal pipe, to improve the draft.

To calculate the amount of stovepipe you will need, measure the distances from the stove to the first elbow and from the elbow to the wall. For the section of pipe that passes through the wall, measure the depth of the wall at a window or door, and add 3 inches. Then measure the distance from this exit point to a point at least 3 feet above the roof line, ending 2 feet above any object within 10 feet.

If the chimney must extend more than 4 feet above the roof, you will need to brace it with lengths of rigid metal conduit, supported by brackets. If the house wall is masonry, you will also have to purchase lead anchors to match the gauge of the fasteners supplied with the chimney supports and connectors.

At the roof line, you can carry the chimney around a shallow eave or, if the overhang is greater than 18 inches, cut through it. For the latter solution you will need to install flashing and a storm collar (page 53, Steps 7 and 8), and a metal spacer to cover the opening in the underside of the overhang. For a shallow overhang of 1 or 2 inches, shift the entire chimney 1 or 2 inches out from the house wall by mounting it on wood blocks bolted to studs in the house framing. For an overhang between 2 and 8 inches deep, route the chimney around the eave with a pair of 15° elbows, as shown below. For the length of the straight section of pipe between the elbows—which depends on the depth of the overhang and the diameter of the pipe—ask your stove dealer.

After you have planned the flue and assembled the parts, begin the installation by cutting the opening in the house wall. If this opening must pass through combustible materials, cut it 4 inches larger than the outside diameter of the insulated pipe. In a masonry wall, the hole can be just large enough for the pipe to pass through.

To cut the opening through wood-frame construction, mark and cut the interior wall surface just as for an opening in a ceiling (page 51, Step 1). To cut through masonry, follow the instructions in Step 1, page 60.

A Smoke Pipe System for Saving Space

A metal chimney outdoors. An exterior wall supports this space-saving metal chimney, which draws hot smoke outdoors and up the side of the house to a safe distance above the roof. Single-walled stovepipe rises from the stove, turns and runs horizontally to the exterior wall; there it connects to a short piece of thicker, insulated chimney pipe that passes through the wall. A wall spacer, nailed to the house siding, separates this exit pipe from wood framing members. An insulated chimney T, attached to the chimney pipe, diverts smoke upward; it rests on a braced platform called a wall support assembly.

Interlocking sections of insulated chimney pipe stacked above the T are reinforced, in this example, with locking bands, similar to automobile hose clamps. Connector bands tie the chimney pipe to the house below and above the 15° elbows that route the pipe around the overhanging eave. A chimney cap tops the system. Not visible here are two collars that fit around the chimney pipe where it pierces the interior wall surface and a removable cleanout cap that snaps into the wall support assembly below the T, to allow the chimney to be cleaned.

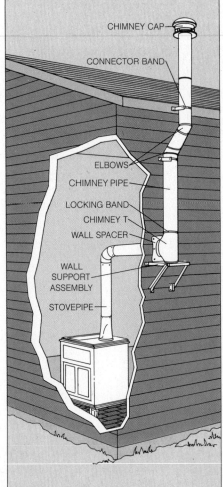

CHIMNEY CAP

CONNECTOR BAND

ELBOWS

CHIMNEY PIPE

LOCKING BAND

CHIMNEY T

WALL SPACER

WALL SUPPORT ASSEMBLY

STOVEPIPE

Running the Flue Out, Then Up

1 **Opening the exterior wall.** Using marker holes drilled at the four corners of the interior opening, draw a guideline for the opening on the exterior wall; cut through the siding and the sheathing with a circular saw. Frame the top and bottom of the opening with 2-by-4s, bracing them against cleats nailed to the flanking studs *(inset)*; toenail the 2-by-4s to the studs. Then frame the sides of the opening with wood strips thick enough to fill the space between the studs and the edge of the opening; nail the strips to the studs in the wall.

2 **Attaching the metal wall spacer.** The wall spacer, designed to keep the insulated pipe centered in the exterior wall opening, must itself be centered over the opening so that the spacer's recessed lip fits against the opening's wood frame. Drive eightpenny (2½-inch) nails through the spacer into the siding at 4-inch intervals, ½ inch in from the spacer edge. Fill any gaps between the spacer and the siding with high-temperature silicone caulk.

3 **Installing the wall support assembly.** Bolt together the parts of the wall support, using the hardware provided, and secure the chimney T to the support plate; this is usually done by fitting the T over a circular collar on the plate. Hold the snout of the T against the wall-spacer opening, using a level to make certain that the top of the T is horizontal; then have a helper make pencil marks through the holes in the support assembly, to locate bolt positions. Re-move the assembly and drill pilot holes for the bolts. Fasten the support and the T to the wall with lag bolts, and snap a metal clean-out cap into the metal collar that extends below the support plate *(inset)*.

If there is an obstruction on the wall below the support plate, assemble the angle-iron braces to slant upward, and connect them to the wall on the sides of the wall spacer.

4 **Adding a locking band.** Push the connecting section of horizontal chimney pipe through the wall from inside the house until it fits inside the snout of the T. Working outside, secure the joint with a locking band, tightening the band ends with the screw and nut provided. Fill any gaps between the chimney pipe and the wall spacer with silicone caulk. Then, working indoors, fill the opening around the pipe with noncombustible ceramic-wool insulation, and slide a trim collar *(see below)* over the pipe. Fasten the collar to the wall, using the screws provided with the collar.

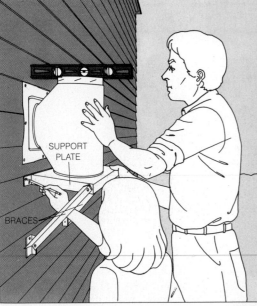

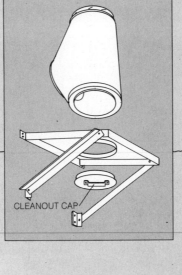

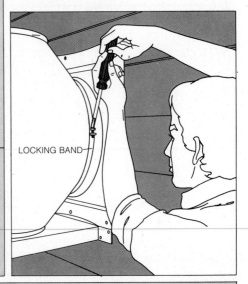

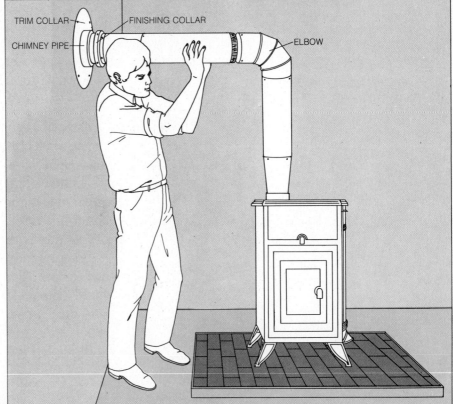

5 **Assembling the stovepipe.** Join the vertical sections of stovepipe leading from the stove to the elbow, with the crimped ends of the pipe sections pointing down toward the stove. Drill three holes at each joint, and fasten the sections with sheet-metal screws. Then slip the finishing collar over an unattached section of pipe, front side of the collar facing the crimped end of the pipe, and slide the smooth end of this pipe section into the chimney pipe in the wall. Join additional sections as necessary, until the horizontal pipe meets the elbow; when the crimped end of this pipe is properly seated in the elbow, the opposite end of the horizontal pipe, at the wall, should extend about 3 inches into the chimney pipe. Fasten the horizontal sections of stovepipe together with sheet-metal screws.

When the entire run of stovepipe has been assembled, slide the finishing collar over the chimney pipe and fasten the collar with screws, first to the stovepipe, then to the chimney pipe.

6 **Anchoring the chimney pipe.** Build the chimney pipe up the side of the house by fastening together successive sections, securing the joints with locking bands. Add a connector band to anchor the pipe to the wall every 8 feet of pipe, as well as below or above an elbow. To position the band, first check to make sure that the chimney is plumb, then tighten the band around the chimney section and mark where the screw holes on the band extensions meet the wall. Remove the band, set aside the uppermost section of the chimney, drill pilot holes at all of the marks, and fasten the band to the siding with screws. Then open the front of the band, and slide the chimney pipe into it. Finally, close the band around the pipe by tightening the bolt and nut at the front opening.

7 **Bypassing the eave.** Slip a 15° elbow onto the last section of pipe. Angle the elbow away from the house wall, and secure it with a locking band. Run the flue away from the house by locking a straight section of pipe onto the angled end of the elbow. Then fasten a second 15° elbow in place to return the flue to vertical.

Install a straight section of chimney pipe onto the top of the second 15° elbow, and fasten it to the fascia with a connector band (Step 6); it may be necessary to screw a wood spacer to the fascia if the fascia and the connector-band extensions do not meet. Continue to add pipe until the chimney extends to the required height above the roof. Add a chimney cap on top of the uppermost section of pipe.

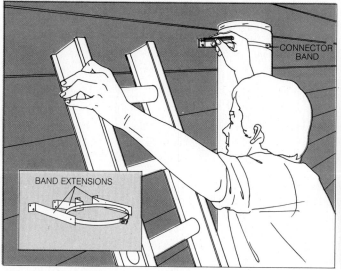

CONNECTOR BAND

BAND EXTENSIONS

FASCIA

Bracing a Tall Chimney Pipe

A well-reinforced chimney. To reinforce a metal chimney that extends more than 4 feet above the roof, brace it with two lengths of ¾-inch aluminum or galvanized-steel electrical conduit. Connect the conduit to the chimney pipe with pipe plates, and attach it to the roof with adjustable roof brackets.

To install the braces, screw the pipe plates to opposite sides of the chimney at the height specified by the manufacturer. Temporarily attach strings to the plates, and angle the strings 60° out from the vertical line of the chimney (top inset) and 30° out from an imaginary perpendicular line midway between the two plates (bottom inset). Where the strings meet the roof, spread a layer of roofing cement and attach the roof brackets. Cut two lengths of conduit to fit between the brackets and the plates. Flatten the brace ends in a vice, then bend the ends of each brace 30° in opposite directions. Drill holes in the brace ends, and bolt the braces in place.

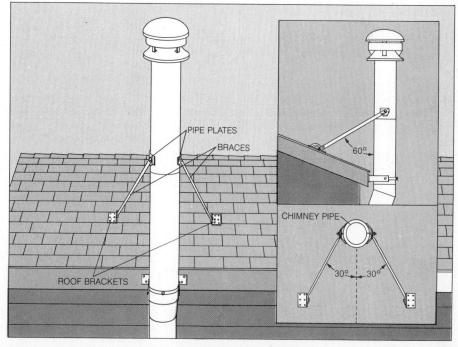

PIPE PLATES

BRACES

ROOF BRACKETS

60°

CHIMNEY PIPE

30° 30°

Recycling an Unused Fireplace

An unused fireplace, even if it has been walled in, can often be salvaged to provide supplementary heat. The fireplace itself presents a ready-made cavity for a metal firebox insert, which is in effect a set-in wood stove. Or the old chimney can be tapped to serve as a flue for a freestanding wood stove. Adapting an open fireplace for a firebox insert is especially easy and results in improved heat efficiency. Inserts are designed to fit into masonry fireboxes and vent directly into the chimney; the only modification required is the removal of the damper plate, to prevent its closing accidentally.

Tapping into the flue of a blocked-off fireplace is harder. You must break through the interior wall, as well as two layers of chimney brick and the flue liner—a time-consuming task that is sometimes, for structural reasons, inadvisable.

Before you use an old fireplace or chimney, it must be inspected, cleaned and put into good working order (pages 14-19 and 120-122). The intensity of the heat produced by a fireplace insert or a freestanding stove is greater than that of an open fireplace, and so the firebox and chimney must be in perfect repair.

Though inserts are made in a range of sizes to fit a variety of fireplace designs, most can be used only with conventional masonry construction, not with prefabricated metal fireboxes. Before shopping for an insert, take precise measurements of the height, width and depth of your firebox. Also record the height and width of the back wall of the firebox; some insert manufacturers specify minimum clearances between the back of the insert and the firebox walls. Use these measurements to select an insert and to fit it with extender panels—metal wings that cover the gaps between the insert and the edges of the fireplace opening. The panels must overlap the firebox mouth by at least 2 inches. Follow the manufacturer's instructions for installation.

Several measurements must also precede the decision to vent a freestanding stove into an unused chimney. First compare the dimensions of the existing flue with the flue size recommended by the stove manufacturer. A chimney flue that is too large will tend to cause draft and creosote-deposit problems; sometimes, though, an oversized flue without bends can be made smaller by the installation of a new liner (pages 23-25).

Tapping into a masonry flue also involves pinpointing the exact location of the flue within the walls of the house, because the hole you cut through the wall and chimney brick must lead directly into the flue. If the fireplace opening is covered and you cannot locate the flue from indoors, climb up on the roof and examine the chimney. First note the position of the flue relative to the chimney structure; a single chimney often has two flues, one venting the furnace heating system, the other the fireplace. Then lower a trouble light into the fireplace flue.

If the light descends unobstructed, the flue is vertical; you can determine its location by measuring from the corner of the house to the center of the flue, then transferring this measurement to the interior wall. Transfer the measurement carefully, remembering to subtract the thickness of the exterior wall from the total figure. The easiest place to measure wall thickness is at an open door or window, taking into account the thickness of any moldings or trim.

If the trouble light does encounter an obstacle, the flue probably is offset to one side. In this case, locating the flue becomes a matter of trial-and-error probes into the chimney or—as a last resort—of reopening the fireplace.

The size of the hole you need to cut is determined by the size of your stovepipe. Add 2 inches to this dimension, to allow for the larger size of the insulated chimney pipe needed to run the flue through the wall. You will not be able to determine the precise length of chimney pipe you need until you have cut into the flue liner (page 61, Step 2). Then measure from the inside of the flue liner to the face of the interior wall. Buy chimney pipe no more than 2 inches longer than the length needed; it cannot be cut.

Finally, observe all code requirements that apply to installing a stove (page 48). Cut the hole for the stovepipe at least 18 inches below the ceiling; and when you are cutting through a combustible wall covering, make the hole large enough so it will clear the insulated chimney pipe by 2 inches all around.

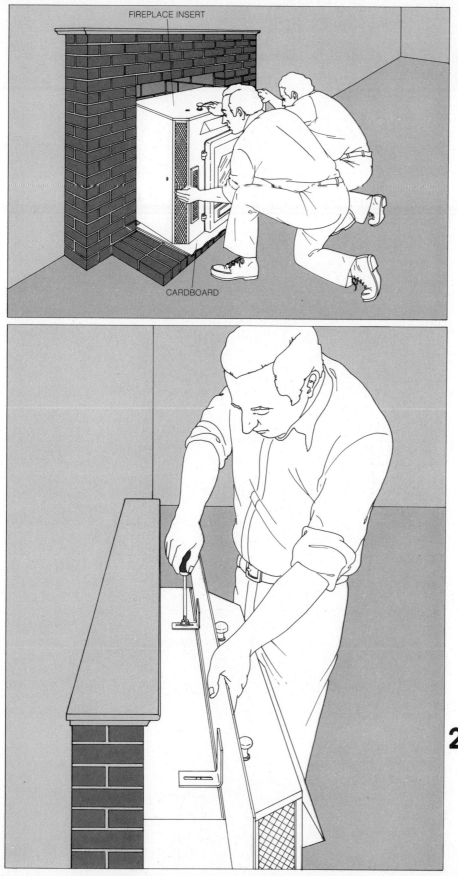

FIREPLACE INSERT

CARDBOARD

Sliding a New Firebox into an Old Fireplace

1 **Positioning the insert.** Remove the damper plate *(page 120)* and lay heavy cardboard over the hearth. Working with a helper, lift the insert onto the hearth and slide it toward the rear wall of the firebox, observing any clearances specified by the manufacturer. Center the unit within the opening. Then, using a level, make sure the two sides of the insert are at the same height. If necessary, adjust the leveling legs at the back of the fireplace insert.

Draw a chalk line across the top of the insert, indicating where the insert lines up with the front of the fireplace opening. Then pull the insert about 8 inches out from the opening.

2 **Adding the extender panels.** Using self-tapping screws, fasten the top extender panel to the insert top by driving the screws, loosely at first, through the predrilled holes. Then shift the slotted brackets of the panel until the back of the panel lines up with the chalk line made in Step 1. Attach the side panels in the same way, lining them up with the top panel. Then tighten all of the screws. If the ends of the top panel protrude beyond the outer edges of the side panels, trim off the protruding ends with a hacksaw.

3 **Caulking and insulating.** Apply a bead of fire-proof silicone caulk along the joints between the insert and the backs of the three extender panels. Also caulk the joints where the top and side panels meet. Then attach 1½-inch-wide strips of insulation (provided with the kit) to the back of the panels, ½ inch inside their outer edges *(inset)*. On some models, the extender panels will have special channels for these bands of insulation. If the insulation strips do not have adhesive backing, cement them in place with a bead of caulk.

With a helper, slide the insert back in the fireplace until the extender panels lie flat against the sides of the opening. Pass a flashlight through the damper at the back of the insert, and place the light on the roof of the insert. Step back and check the installation for light leakage at the edges of the extender panels and at the joints between the panels and the insert. If there are any gaps, pull the insert out and add more caulk or insulation. On some inserts, the bottom is not insulated, and you may have to add a lining of firebrick *(page 28)*. Remove the cardboard.

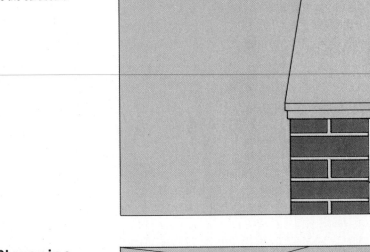
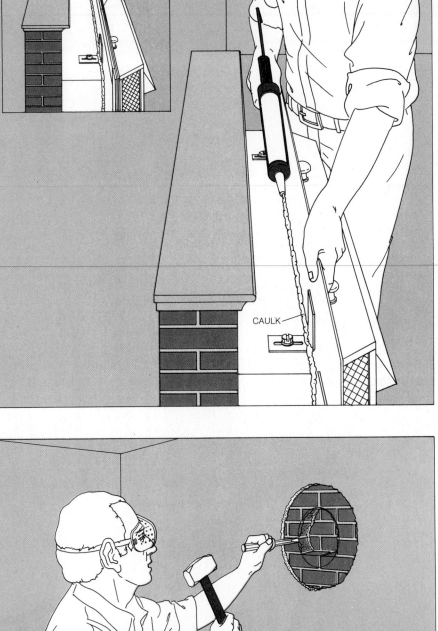

INSULATION

CAULK

Connecting a Stovepipe with a Masonry Chimney

1 **Cutting through the masonry.** Expose the chimney bricks in a circular area 4 inches larger than the diameter of the insulated chimney pipe, and draw a circle the diameter of the pipe in the center of that area. Using a drill fitted with a masonry bit, loosen the mortar around the bricks within the circle. Extract the whole bricks at the center of the circle; then, with a masonry chisel and small sledge, chip away the remaining bricks, slowly roughing out the opening.

If your chimney has a double wall of bricks, cut through the second wall in the same way. If there is rubble between the brick wall and the terra-cotta flue lining, clear it away. Again mark the circle, this time on the flue-liner wall.

2 Piercing the flue liner. Drill holes at ½-inch intervals inside the circumference of the circle, tilting the drill at a slight angle, if necessary, to avoid hitting the bricks around the opening. Gently tap the circle with a ball-peen hammer, to break the flue liner along the perforations. If the liner does not come out in one piece, drill additional holes and remove the terra-cotta in sections to clear the circular opening. Nibble away any rough edges with tile nippers.

Measure the distance from the face of the interior wall to the inside surface of the flue liner. Buy insulated chimney pipe no more than 2 inches longer than this measurement.

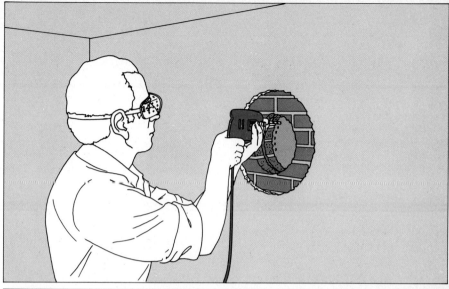

3 Installing the chimney pipe. Position the chimney pipe inside the hole, so that its flanged end is flush with the inside face of the flue and its collar end extends no more than 2 inches out from the interior wall. Reaching through the pipe, use your fingers to build up a ring of special fireplace mortar between the flange and the flue-liner wall, closing any gaps between the pipe and the flue wall. Place a tube of special fireplace mortar in a caulking gun, and force the mortar into any gaps between the pipe and the brick walls of the chimney. Be sure to leave at least 2 inches of space between the chimney pipe and the edge of the finished wall.

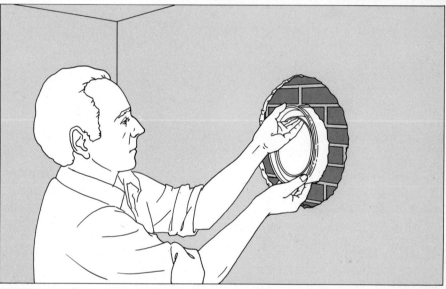

4 Disguising the hole. Use a narrow finishing collar and a wide trim collar to cover the opening in the wall. First attach the finishing collar to the end of the chimney pipe, driving sheet-metal screws through the predrilled holes in the collar and against the pipe. Then slip the trim collar over the finishing collar, and mark the position of pilot holes for the four screws that will attach the collar to the wall. Drill ¼-inch holes at these marks, and fasten the trim collar to the wall with screws supplied with the collar.

Install the stove as described on pages 48-57. Fit the stovepipe into the insulated chimney pipe, securing it by means of screws through the flange of the finishing collar.

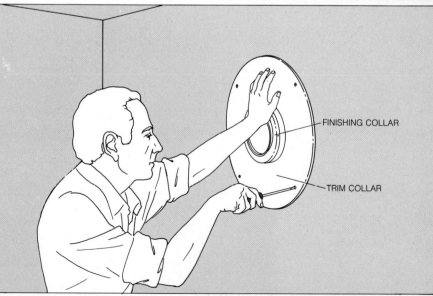

FINISHING COLLAR

TRIM COLLAR

Prefab Fireplaces: Efficient and Easy to Install

If you long for the cheeriness of an open fire but want the heating efficiency of a wood stove, a prefabricated fireplace may be your answer. When these pre-assembled units are built into the wall, they closely resemble conventional fireplaces; but they can be installed with a fraction of the labor and cost. Other versions, such as the one shown on page 67, are freestanding and are truly a cross between a fireplace and a stove. The major difference between them and a stove is that the freestanding prefabs have glass or metal-mesh doors.

Prefabs designed to be built into a wall are known as zero-clearance fireplaces. They are heavily insulated and can be placed directly against a combustible surface without fire danger. This insulation, plus an airtight firebox, makes a zero-clearance fireplace very efficient: A well-designed one, used with its doors shut, matches a wood stove in efficiency.

In addition, many prefab fireplaces come with a range of options to increase their heating potential. Some models draw in cool air from the room, circulate it around the firebox, then release the heated air back into the room. Others have air-intake ducts that bring in air from outside the house to improve combustion in the firebox. The hot-air ducts on some models direct fireplace heat into the room and can be given duct extensions to channel heat into other rooms.

Installation of a prefab fireplace is relatively simple. You will need a screwdriver, a saber saw and a drill to hook up air ducts and a flue and to fasten the unit to the floor. You will have to frame a built-in unit with a new wall to make it look part of the room. But you will not have to reinforce the floor as you would for a masonry fireplace; prefabs are comparatively light, weighing between 200 and 500 pounds. Neither will you have to provide insulation between the floor and the unit. Models approved by the Underwriters Laboratories will satisfy the fire-safety requirements of most local building codes, although it is best to check your local code when you apply for a permit for the job.

The stud wall that frames a prefab fireplace can be faced with plywood, paneling , wallboard, brick, stone veneer or any of the materials discussed on pages 108-115. Noncombustible materials, such as brick or stone, can overlap the metal face around the firebox; the maker's directions tell how far these materials must be set back from the firebox opening.

A noncombustible material is necessary for the hearth also. Prefabricated hearths are available; you can also lay brick, slate, marble or flagstone in front of the opening. As an alternative to the common installation at floor level, a prefab fireplace can be elevated on a platform. A simple boxlike frame built of 2-by-4s surmounted by a ⅝-inch plywood top is strong enough to support such a unit. The bottom of the frame should be nailed to the floor, the back of the frame to studs in the wall; additional 2-by-4s, spaced at 16-inch intervals, should brace the frame for additional support.

A prefab must be connected to flue pipe that is sold with the fireplace unit. The pipe ordinarily requires only a 2-inch clearance from combustible framing materials and wall surfaces, and it is installed in much the same way as a flue for a wood stove (pages 48-57). To angle the interior pipe around ceiling joists or other obstacles, 15° and 30° elbows are available. But be sure to check the location of joists, studs, wiring and ducts in both the walls and the ceiling before deciding where to put the fireplace or cutting into a wall.

A prefab can be installed flush with a wall, offset from it, or across a corner, as explained opposite. Because of the danger of heat and sparks, however, the firebox opening should be at least 36 inches from any wall perpendicular to it. Also, it is always simpler to install the fireplace against an exterior wall. Before beginning the job, pry off the baseboards along the wall against which the unit will be installed. They can later be cut to length and nailed back in place to make the fireplace look truly built in.

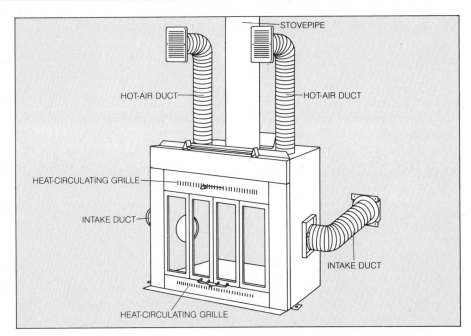

Anatomy of a prefab fireplace. This built-in fireplace is a triple-walled trapezoidal box lined with insulation and firebrick. Folding glass doors seal off the firebox from the room it faces, reducing the loss of warm air up the chimney; but the doors can be opened and a metal-mesh screen used when you want the effect of an open fire. Air from the room is drawn in through the heat-circulating grille below the firebox, is heated as it circulates in a chamber surrounding the firebox, then escapes back into the room through the grille near the top of the unit. Two optional features are the hot-air ducts, which disperse additional warm air into the room from registers built in above the fireplace, and cold-air intake ducts, which direct outside air into the firebox to feed the fire. A triple-walled chimney pipe and built-in insulation keep the outside cool.

Three Installations for a Fully Insulated Unit

One fireplace, three ways. The position of a zero-clearance fireplace is dictated by convenience and the esthetics of the room. In a full-projection installation *(top)*, three new walls jut into the room, enclosing the fireplace against an existing wall. The fireplace can also be built into a corner *(center)*, out of the flow of traffic. Here the corner fireplace has been installed on a platform, raising it off the floor. If floor space is at a premium, the fireplace can be installed flush against an exterior wall *(bottom)*, with the firebox resting on a concrete pad outside the house. In this installation, an enclosure called a chase is built outside the wall to house both the fireplace and the chimney pipe.

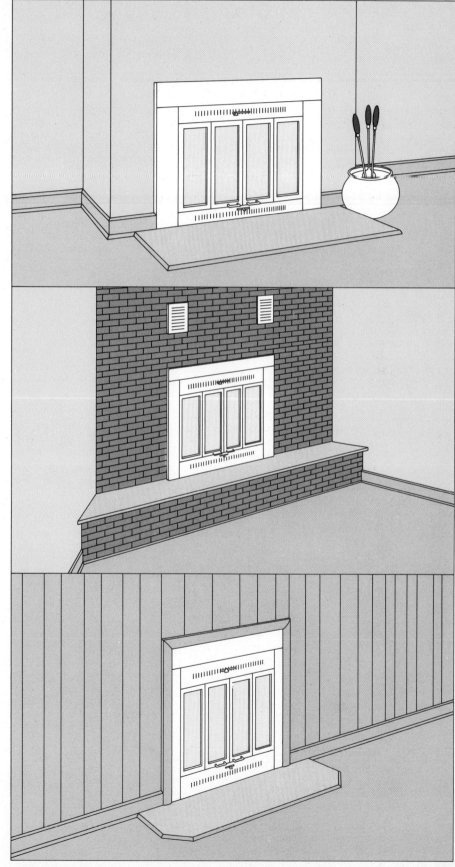

A Projecting Prefab up against the Wall

1 **Positioning the fireplace.** Lift the firebox into place against an exterior wall, and slide the 3-inch-wide spark-guard strip of metal halfway under the front of the firebox. Using the screws supplied by the manufacturer, anchor the side hold-down brackets to the floor.

To locate access holes for the air-intake ducts, mark the wall 18½ inches up from the floor midway between the first pair of studs on each side of the fireplace. Using an electric drill fitted with a long bit, drill through the inside and outside walls at each mark. Then, on each side, hold one leg of a compass at the hole while you scribe a 4½-inch-diameter circle around it, on both the inside and the outside wall surfaces.

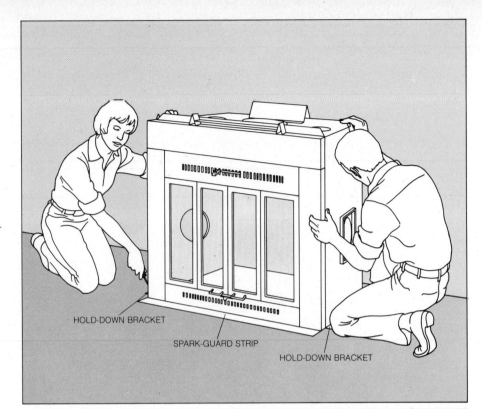

HOLD-DOWN BRACKET

SPARK-GUARD STRIP

HOLD-DOWN BRACKET

2 **Cutting the air-intake duct openings.** Drill a ½-inch hole just inside the circumference of one of the circles marked on the house exterior, and use it as a point of entry for a keyhole saw or an electric saber saw. Cut along the circle through both the siding and the sheathing. Repeat, cutting out the remaining circles inside and outside the house. Remove any insulation to clear a path through the two openings in the wall. Slide a vent assembly for the air-intake duct into each exterior hole, and attach the assembly to the siding with screws (inset).

Install vent assemblies that will carry the chimney pipe either through the outside wall, as shown on page 54, or through the ceiling and roof, as shown on page 49.

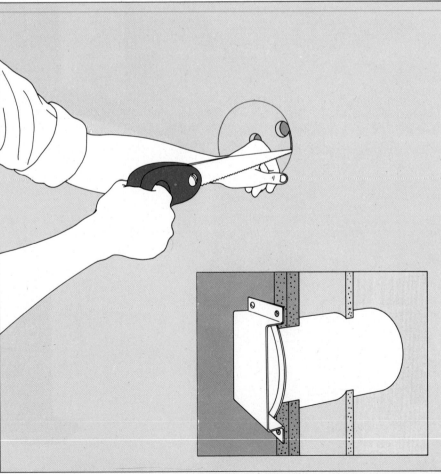

3 **Installing the cold-air ducts.** Using a hose clamp, attach one end of a flexible metal air duct to the built-in duct collar on one side of the firebox. Attach the other end of the duct to the vent assembly installed in Step 2, again using a hose clamp. Wrap the duct with fiberglass insulation, taping it in place. Install a duct on the other side of the fireplace in the same manner.

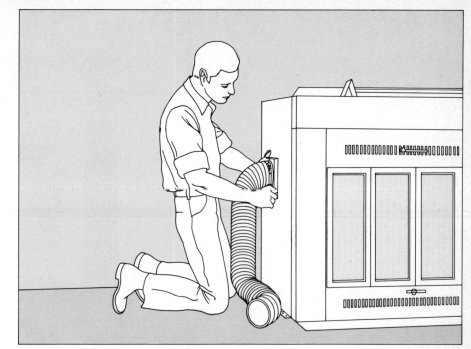

4 **Connecting the flue and hot-air ducts.** Fit a length of chimney pipe over the flue collar on the top of the fireplace, aligning the pipe seam with the notch on the back of the collar. Attach the pipe to the collar with self-tapping metal screws. Add lengths of pipe to extend the flue to the roof or to the outside wall. Then, using conventional chimney pipe, extend the flue 3 feet above the roof, as shown on page 53.

To attach the hot-air ducts, remove the two knockout plates on the top of the fireplace and lift out the perforated disk of insulation at the top of the air-circulating chamber. Fit the duct collars supplied with the fireplace into these openings. Align the holes in the collar with the holes in the fireplace top, and secure the collars with screws *(inset)*. Then pull back the insulation sleeve on each duct, and attach each duct to its collar with a hose clamp; slide the insulation back over the clamps.

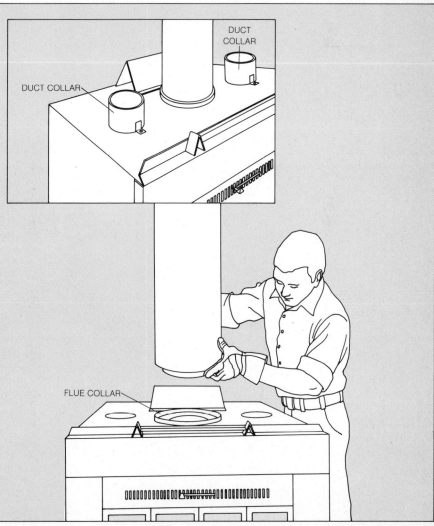

DUCT COLLAR

DUCT COLLAR

FLUE COLLAR

Enclosing with Stud Walls

Creating a false wall. The stud wall framing this full-projection prefab fireplace is made
of 2-by-4s and consists of a top plate that is
nailed to ceiling joists, a sole plate that is nailed
to the floor, and studs spaced at 12-inch intervals and toenailed between the plates. The studs
against the existing wall are nailed to studs
in that wall. A header made of two 2-by-4s nailed
face to face is just above the fireplace, butt-
nailed through the studs on each side and supported at its ends by short jack studs. The
two framed openings for hot-air ducts should be
at least 18 inches below the ceiling; the top
and bottom frames are 12½ inches apart and are
butt-nailed to flanking studs.

The stud framing is recessed from the face of
the fireplace by the thickness of the wallboard or
paneling selected to cover the wall. The ends
of the hot-air ducts should be pulled through their
openings before the wall covering is applied.
After the wall covering is in place, small gaps between this covering and the fireplace are filled
with noncombustible caulk, and the gaps are then
hidden by decorative molding.

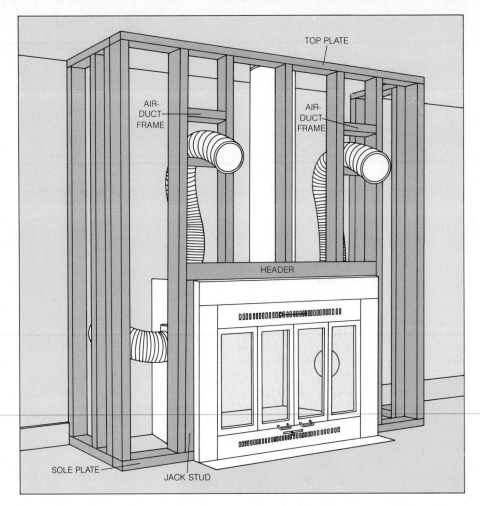

Registers and the Hearth

Setting in the duct registers. To mount each
register box, first nail the two shields provided
with the box to the sides of the duct opening,
leaving enough space between the shields and the
wall surface to accommodate the tabs at the
top and bottom of the box. Then, with a hose
clamp, connect a duct to the flange on the
back of the box; to make this connection, pull
back the duct insulation an inch or two and
replace it when the clamp is secure. Using pliers,
bend the two metal tabs at the top of the register box and hook them over the shields. Fit the
box into the opening, bend the lower tabs and
hook them under the bottom of the shields. Screw
the register grille in place, louvers angled
so that they will direct heat downward *(inset)*.

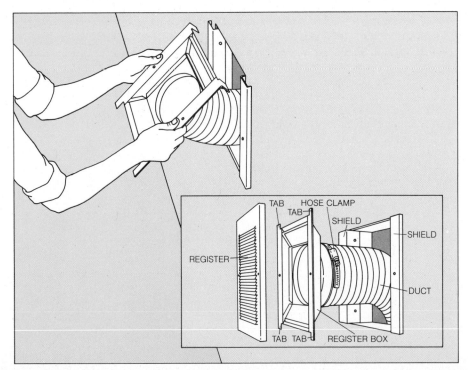

Laying the hearth. Center a hearthstone in front of the fireplace, and trim its edges with quarter-round molding. Miter the corners of the molding pieces, and nail them to the floor with sixpenny finishing nails driven at a 45° angle.

The hearthstone must be at least ⅜ inch thick; it should extend 18 inches out from the front of the fireplace opening and 12 inches to either side. If you choose to use slate or marble for the hearth, you must handle it with care, because it is quite fragile *(page 109)*.

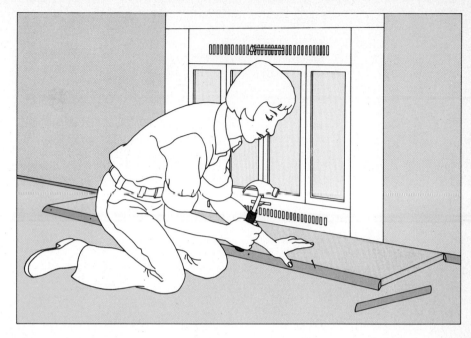

That Funnel-Shaped Freestanding Fireplace

Another type of prefabricated fireplace that is particularly popular is the freestanding metal fireplace with a funnel-shaped hood. This is the fireplace that conjures up images of ski lodges and chic backwoods cabins. Such prefabs come in a spectrum of baked-enamel colors as well as a range of unfinished metals that includes brass, copper, stainless steel and iron.

Most of these fireplaces are broad cones, designed to be placed near the middle of a room, but some models have built-in heat shields to permit installation within a few inches of a wall or in a corner. Typically these fireplaces are set on a noncombustible hearth. However, some models are suspended, hanging from the ceiling beams on heavy chains; a hearth is still necessary beneath a suspended fireplace. The hearth can be anything from a slab of bricks to a metal ring filled with 2 inches of small stones or marble chips.

A freestanding fireplace is the nearest thing there is to an instant fireplace. The only complicated part of the installation job is erecting the prefabricated chimney *(page 48)*. Once this is done, the factory-assembled firebox is moved into place and connected to the chimney with stovepipe. On some models,

you will need to protect the bottom of the firebox with a lining of heat-resistant material to prevent the metal from overheating and cracking. This material comes with the unit in powdered form, to be mixed with water and troweled in to a depth of 2 inches. On other models, the firebox comes lined.

Unlike their close cousin, the zero-clearance fireplace, most freestanding fireplaces lack built-in insulation. But this very lack of insulation makes them excellent radiators of heat—they are considerably more efficient than masonry fireplaces. Additional heat-conservation features found on some units are glass doors, to seal off the firebox and prevent the loss of room heat up the flue, and electric blowers to force heated air into the room.

One drawback of some freestanding fireplaces is their susceptibility to vagaries in the draft that feeds the fire. Just walking close to such a fireplace may disrupt the draft enough to divert smoke into the room. When evenness of draft is a problem, an air-intake duct often can be installed in the floor to feed outside air into the firebox, thus bypassing the need for room air.

Because they lack built-in insulation, freestanding fireplaces must be in-

stalled at least 36 inches from the wall; the manufacturer's directions will specify the necessary clearance. But clearance may also be dictated by your local building code; before buying such a unit, check your local code requirements. Generally, the firebox must rest on a ⅜-inch-thick noncombustible hearth that extends 18 inches in front of the fireplace opening and 8 inches to each side. The stovepipe usually must have 18 inches of clearance.

3

A Fireplace of Brick and Mortar

Building a heatproof floor. Speckled fire-bricks, containing special mineral additives designed to help them withstand the intense heat of the firebox in a fireplace, are dry-fitted over a concrete slab to form the firebox floor. Spaced ⅛ inch apart, they will later be mortared in place with a 9-inch spade-shaped mason's trowel. When the bricks must be cut to fit around openings for an ashpit and an air inlet, the sharp end of a bricklayer's hammer is used to score a fracture line, then the blunt end is used to break off the unwanted pieces.

As mankind must surely have discovered early on, it is no mean trick to design an indoor fire enclosure that extracts the most heat from the least fuel and at the same time completely disposes of the smoke. But the fireplace described in this chapter accomplishes exactly that, and something equally admirable: It can be built into an exterior wall with minimum alteration to the house. Its design is the result of centuries of trial and error, as well as of changing concepts of a fireplace's function.

The fireplace was once an integral part of domestic life. It was used for cooking as well as for heating, and it was therefore large enough to accommodate pots and kettles suspended from swinging iron brackets, a built-in oven and even a spit for roasting meat. Cottage crafts were dependent on it: The fire's heat was used for making candles and dyeing cloth, and its by-products—smoke and vast quantities of ashes—were used to cure meat and make soap.

But as domestic architecture evolved from multipurpose to single-purpose rooms, the character of the fireplace changed too. It became smaller and shallower and was used exclusively for heating; in this capacity, it became the subject of scientific scrutiny in an effort to improve its efficiency. The fireplace also became the decorative focus of the room.

Many modern fireplaces have a feature that was part of the old kitchen hearth: an ashpit, the chamber under the hearth for collecting ashes. Today's fireplaces may also contain two devices that appeared in differing form in the 18th Century: a hinged metal chimney damper, and a special air inlet to improve combustion. Benjamin Franklin described the prototypes of both. One was a damper that consisted of an iron frame with a plate that slid "backwards and forwards in the grooves on each side of the plate." The other device was a German contrivance meant to provide more air for the fire. A metal duct built into the top part of a window, it was called a "was-ist-das" by the French—supposedly the question people asked when they first saw it.

Various other ingenious gadgets have been appended to the fireplace—a double-decker firebox, a pull-out cast-iron firebox, a revolving firebox for servants to start fires in an adjacent room, and a kind of roll-top chimney breast for blocking smoke. But the greatest improvement in fireplace design was the reinvention by the British in the 15th Century of Roman clay bricks and lime-based mortar. Today the brick-and-mortar chimney, with its superb fire resistance, is taken for granted—yet as recently as American Colonial times chimneys often were precariously made of wattle and daub, a tapered wooden frame of interwoven twigs coated inside and out with mud.

The Strategy of Building a Masonry Tower

Constructing a masonry fireplace from the ground up is arguably the most ambitious job a homeowner can undertake, but careful planning and attention to detail will dispel the mysteries. The planning is first of all structural. A fireplace is basically a freestanding masonry tower; it does not depend on the house for support, and its component parts must therefore be tightly linked with mortar, masonry ties and steel reinforcing rods. It must also be strong; the foundation footing for a typical single-story fireplace supports a weight of 11 tons.

Besides being strong, the fireplace must be proportioned to cater to the physical needs of burning wood and exploit the heat that results (*pages 8-11*). This delicate trade-off is best achieved by maintaining the space relationships shown in the chart below and drawings opposite. The drawings are intended only as a starting point, to help you understand the interlocking functions of all parts of the fireplace and to guide you in the creation of your own design.

In addition to planning the structure of the fireplace, you must also decide on its finishing materials in advance. Brick, stucco, tile, marble, slate, stone and wood all are optional choices for the facing, the hearth and the mantel. The thickness of these materials must be part of your preliminary calculations.

When a fireplace is added to an existing structure, problems of placement arise that must also be resolved in the planning stage. An exterior wall is the most logical site, since this location entails the least structural disturbance. But a fireplace should also be clear of doors and hallways that might produce drafts, and if possible, it should be located where rerouting of electric wires, plumbing or ductwork will not be required. Fireplace location also affects the height of the chimney. Most codes require a chimney to be 2 feet higher than any structure within 10 feet, including the sloping roof of your own house.

Before you begin construction, assemble all the materials you will need in order to avoid delays that might expose the project to weather damage. To estimate the number of bricks required, calculate the square footage of all the brick surfaces, taking into account that many of the brick walls are double-thick. Multiply this figure by 6.66—the number of standard bricks per square foot of wall—and add 5 per cent to this amount to allow for breakage. For the concrete-block foundation walls, multiply the estimated square footage by 1.13—the number of blocks per square foot—and buy enough extra to fill in the foundation core.

The number of firebricks needed varies with the configuration of the firebox, but it seldom is more than the 64 bricks used for the average 29-by-36-by-16-inch firebox shown here. The terra-cotta flue liners are usually 2 feet long; buy enough to cover the distance from the top of the smoke chamber to a point 8 inches above the rim of the chimney.

Concrete blocks and standard bricks are set in masonry mortar; firebricks and flue liners are set in a special fireplace mortar, which is also used to coat the inside of the smoke chamber. Masonry mortar comes in 72-pound bags; you will need 7½ bags for every 1,000 bricks and one bag for every 50 concrete blocks. Add about 10 per cent to this total for odd jobs, such as stabilizing rubble between the walls of the firebox. Fireplace mortar, often called refractory cement, comes ready-mixed in 1-gallon cans. You will need 4 to 5 gallons for a 29-by-36-by-16-inch firebox, a smoke chamber and the connecting joints between 10 feet of flue. To estimate the amount of concrete you will need for the foundation footing and hearth slab, measure the cubic feet of space each will occupy, keeping in mind that the depth of the footing is usually determined by building codes.

Among the nonmasonry components that you should have on hand are the damper, the steel lintels used in the foundations and the fireplace proper, and covers for the ash dump and the air intake. Other materials that should be ordered in advance are the plywood and reinforcing bars used in the poured-concrete hearth slab and the foundation footing, and the silicone caulk and metal flashing that finish the chimney.

One final word of caution: When the fireplace is complete, wait two weeks before building a fire.

Dimensions That Ensure Fireplace Efficiency

Proportions of a fireplace. Dimensions that affect fireplace efficiency are listed across the top of this chart. The heights and widths in the first two columns reflect the most common sizes of fireplace openings. For the fireplace to operate at peak efficiency, the dimensions in the next six columns must be proportioned to the size of this opening. The final column gives the header height, which is the height of the opening you will have to cut through the wall.

Firebox width	Firebox height	Firebox depth	Fireback width	Fireback height	Height to damper	Damper width	Flue-liner dimensions	Height to header
26	24	16	13	14	32	8¾	8 x 12	52
28	24	16	15	14	32	8¾	8 x 12	52
30	29	16	17	14	37	8¾	13 x 13	57
32	29	16	19	14	37	8¾	13 x 13	57
36	29	16	23	14	37	8¾	13 x 13	57
40	29	16	27	14	37	8¾	12 x 16	57
42	32	16	29	14	40	8¾	16 x 16	60

All dimensions are expressed in inches.

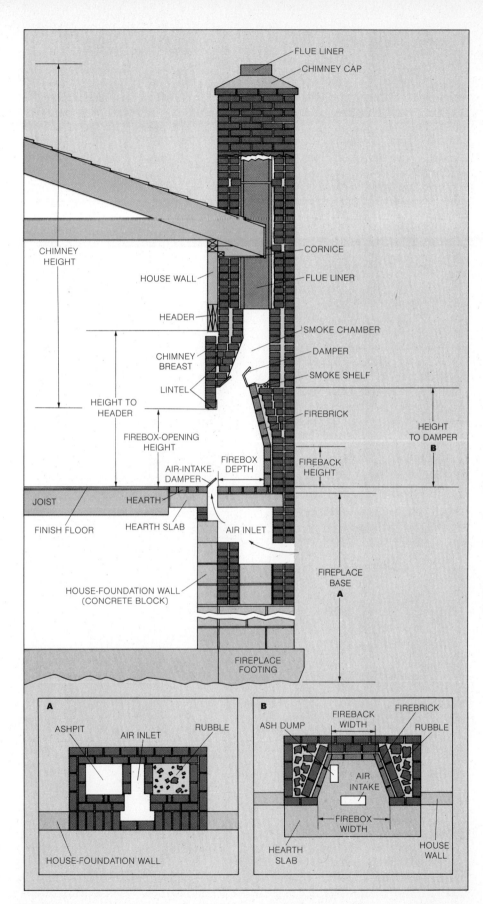

The Shapes and Vents That Make a Fireplace Work

Anatomy of a fireplace addition. As seen in the cross section, a freestanding masonry fireplace can be added to a house with relatively little disturbance to the existing structure. The base of the fireplace butts against the house foundation and rises beside it to first-floor level, where the floor joists are cut away and boxed to accommodate the front of the hearth slab. An opening is also cut through the exterior wall at this level for the firebox and the chimney breast above it. A header of doubled 2-inch lumber, installed above this opening, supports the weight of the house above. The chimney butts against the sheathing on the side of the house, up as far as the cornice and the roof, and then it passes through both of these.

The base of the fireplace, resting on a concrete footing, is made of concrete block and has hollow sections for an ashpit and an air inlet *(top view, inset A)*. From slightly below ground level, the base is enclosed by a double layer of bricks, which continues—above the firebox— all the way to the chimney cap. The base is topped by a poured-concrete hearth slab, which is covered by a layer of firebrick before the firebox is built atop it. Around the firebox the wall is triple-thick and is further buffered with masonry rubble *(top view, inset B)*. Above the firebox, the damper and the smoke shelf form the bottom of the smoke chamber, whose three sloping sides rise to the point where the interior bricks support the first flue liner of the chimney. The flue liners are stacked up to and slightly beyond the chimney top, where the final liner is surrounded by the sloping chimney cap.

Dimensions critical to the efficiency of this fireplace are given on the main drawing and the insets. Relative proportions for these fireplace parts are listed in the chart opposite.

Mastering the Fundamental Bricklaying Skills

By the time you finish building a fireplace, you probably will have mixed more mortar and laid more bricks than you will care to remember. But the importance of these basic tasks must not be taken lightly. The life expectancy of the finished product will be directly proportional to the quality and consistency of your workmanship.

The special fireplace mortar that bonds firebricks and flue liner is always a factory-mixed slurry. But for other mortars and all concrete, buy the ingredients and make your own mixtures. By doing so, you can regulate the size of the batches, mixing only what you can conveniently use, and thereby avoid waste.

Concrete for the foundation footing and hearth slab must be mixed in fairly large quantities: Each of these structural elements is poured all at once. A wheelbarrow is the usual mixing and pouring container, but it holds only about 2½ cubic feet of concrete. A typical fireplace uses about 18 cubic feet for the footing and 10 cubic feet for the hearth. You can mix several batches in rapid succession or rent a power mixer.

To measure the ingredients for the concrete, use a plastic bucket marked off in gallons. The standard recipe for 1 cubic foot of concrete calls for 1⅝ gallons of portland cement, 3¼ gallons of dry building sand, 6 gallons of ¾-inch gravel aggregate and 1½ gallons of water.

The mortar used to bond bricks and concrete blocks is also mixed in a wheelbarrow, but about 1 cubic foot at a time—enough to lay approximately 30 bricks or 16 standard (8-inch) concrete blocks. First combine 2½ gallons of masonry cement and 7½ gallons of building sand. Then add water gradually, in small amounts, until the mortar is completely free of lumps: For bricks, mortar should have the consistency of soft mush; for blocks, it should be stiffer.

The art of laying bricks is explained below and at right. Bricks in a fireplace should be arranged in a running-bond pattern, with each brick equally overlapping the vertical mortar joint of the two bricks below. Concrete blocks should also be laid in this pattern, but the task of spreading mortar on the edges of a hollow block is necessarily more painstaking

than "throwing" mortar on bricks. To build up mortar on the narrow edges of a block, trowel it on a little at a time. With both bricks and blocks, mortar joints should be ⅜ inch wide.

In many cases, during the construction of the fireplace you will have to cut bricks and blocks to size. For this you will need a bricklayer's hammer, a ball-peen hammer and a 4-inch-wide chisel called a brickset. Except when done by an experienced mason, cutting masonry is at best unpredictable. Do not despair if an occasional brick shatters or splits unevenly— the shards from your failed efforts will serve as rubble in the walls of the fireplace. But be sure to wear safety goggles whenever you cut brick or block.

You may also have to trim down a section of the terra-cotta flue liner. A circular saw equipped with an abrasive masonry blade is the best tool for this job. Wear goggles and a respirator when you saw through masonry.

When the walls of the fireplace extend beyond your reach, you will have to erect a scaffold, as shown on page 75. Rental outlets usually provide pipe scaffolding.

Laying a Course of Brick

1 **Throwing a line of mortar.** Scoop up enough mortar to half-fill the trowel blade, then snap the trowel sharply downward to compact the load. Set the point of the trowel, face up, against the end of the last brick laid, then slide the trowel along the top of the course below as you rotate the blade forward 180°. A properly loaded and handled trowel will deposit a 1-inch-thick layer of mortar across the top of three or four bricks.

2 **Furrowing the mortar.** Immediately draw the point of the trowel along the center of the mortar bed just thrown. This creates a small furrow that spreads the mortar slightly toward the edges of the bricks, distributing the mortar evenly for the next course of bricks.

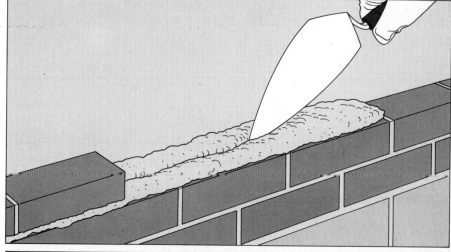

3 **Buttering the interior bricks.** For every brick not at the end of a row, scoop up enough mortar to cover one end of the brick with ¾ inch of mortar. Spread the mortar with the trowel, using the edge of the trowel to remove any excess that slides onto the face of the brick.

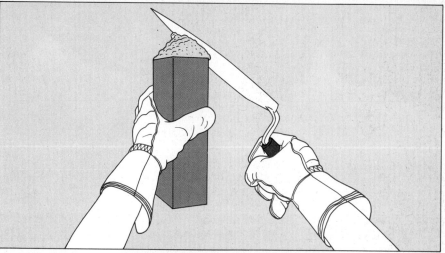

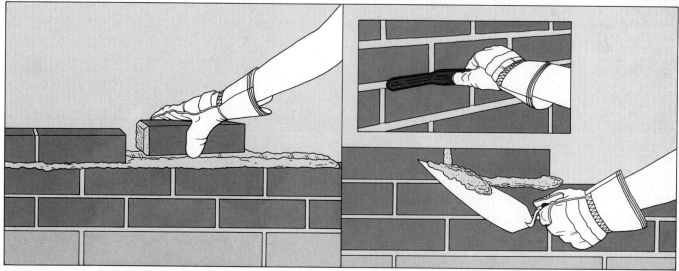

4 **Laying the brick.** Place the brick in the bed of mortar, with its buttered end facing the preceding brick *(above, left)*. In one motion, force the brick down into the mortar bed and against the preceding brick, until the vertical and horizontal joints between the bricks are a uniform ⅜ inch thick and the face of the brick just touches the mason's line (omitted here for clarity). With the edge of the trowel, scrape off any excess mortar. After five or six courses, use a joining tool to compress the mortar joints, shaping them into concave coves *(inset, above right)*.

Cutting a Brick Down to Size

Cutting across a brick. After penciling a cutting line on all sides of the brick but its face, rest the brick on the ground, or on a stack of newspapers if you are working inside the house. Score along the line with a brickset *(below, left)*, facing the bevel of the brickset toward the waste portion of the brick and tapping on its handle with a ball-peen hammer. Working around the brick, gradually deepen each of the scored lines until the brick splits in two. Use the curved chisel end of a bricklayer's hammer to chip off any ragged edges of brick that may remain after the brick has been split *(below, right)*, so that the cut surface of the brick will be as flat as you can make it.

Cutting a brick lengthwise. Pencil a continuous cutting line along the four edges of the brick, and mark the center point of the line on one long edge. Score the line by tapping along it with the sharp edge of the square end of a bricklayer's hammer. Then grip the brick firmly in one hand and strike the center point sharply with the flat surface of the hammer, bringing the hammer down just to one side of the scored line; the brick should split in two.

If the brick does not break, deepen the scored line—you may need to deepen the line with a brickset, using the technique shown at far left. After the brick splits, use the chisel end of the hammer to smooth the cut surface.

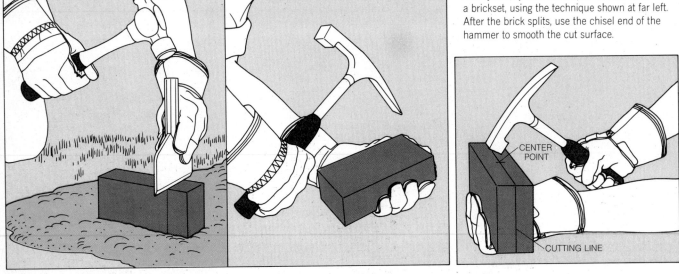

Trimming a Concrete Block

Cutting a block. Use a brickset and a ball-peen hammer to cut, in stages, through the walls of the block, following a guideline placed at the desired length—but do not attempt to cut over an inner partition. If necessary, cut in from both ends of the block in order to avoid the partitions. Hold the brickset with its beveled edge toward the waste side of the block; tap lightly along the line on one side of the block after another, gradually deepening the cut. When the block is split, use a bricklayer's hammer to chip away the ragged edges *(above, right)*.

Tailoring a Terra-cotta Flue Liner with a Saw

Cutting with a masonry blade. To cut a flue liner using a circular saw, mark a line around the walls of the liner and adjust the saw to cut no more than ⅜ inch deep. Start the saw with its blade clear of the liner; then move the blade slowly along the cutting line, scoring the liner. When one side is scored, turn off the saw and rotate the liner; again start the saw clear of the liner. When you have scored all four sides, lower the blade another ⅜ inch and repeat the procedure. Increase the blade depth in ⅜-inch increments until you have cut through the liner.

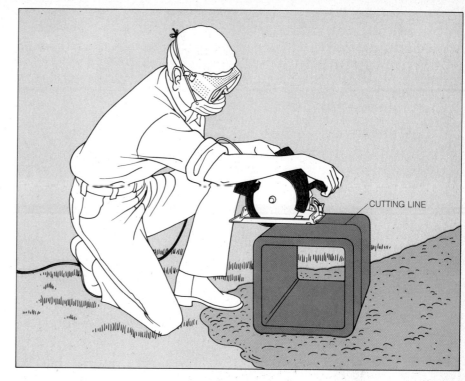

CUTTING LINE

A Solid Perch for Work off the Ground

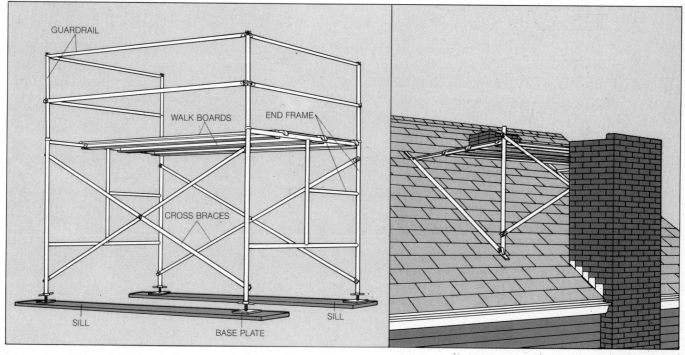

GUARDRAIL

WALK BOARDS

END FRAME

CROSS BRACES

SILL

BASE PLATE

SILL

Two types of mason's scaffolding. The legs of a modular pipe structure *(left)* are equipped with adjustable base plates that should rest on 2-by-12 planks, called sills, on the ground. The welded frames at each end of the scaffold incorporate ladders and are held upright by cross-bracing pipes. The cross braces are bolted together at their intersections and are connected to the end frames with coupling pins. Aluminum-framed plywood planks, called walk boards, hook over the tops of the end frames to serve as the working platform. A guardrail on three sides fits into the top ends of the end-frame pipes.

The base plates can be elevated individually to level the assembly. Extra end-frame sections— with their own cross braces—can be added on top of the first set to increase the height of the platform. The mason's roof scaffolding *(right)* adjusts to any slope and supports walk boards with its pipe frame and cross braces. The frame member that clings to the roof has a flat end that slides under a shingle and is nailed into a rafter with 16-penny (3½-inch) nails.

Building a Base to Support Several Tons

On a drive through the countryside, it is not uncommon to see an old chimney standing upright amid the rubble of a fire-gutted farmhouse. The sight, though strange, is in fact a testimony to the strength and independence of the fireplace structure. No matter where the fireplace is located in the house, its masonry rises from belowground to above the roof independent of the house walls, standing steady while the walls shift, settle or even burn around it.

The key to the remarkable stability of the fireplace is the solid base that supports it. The base begins with a reinforced concrete footing that supports several courses of thick-walled concrete blocks—called semisolid blocks. Above the blocks, the base continues upward with double courses of brick that at a certain level form the chimney walls. Just below the firebox, the brickwork is topped off with a reinforced concrete slab that supports both the firebox and the chimney and extends into the house to support the hearth.

Because the design and dimensions of the base must coordinate perfectly with the design and dimensions of the firebox and the chimney, planning the base is a crucial part of its construction. Use the guidelines on pages 70 and 71 to determine the proper sizes for all three.

Also check your local building code before you begin. The code will probably require that the concrete footing—like any other foundation—must be poured below the average depth of frost in your climate zone. In addition, if the backfill around the house is sandy or recently added, codes will usually require that the footing for an appended fireplace be placed at least as deep as the footing of the house foundation.

For a one-story exterior chimney such as the one on page 71, most codes require a footing 12 inches thick and wide enough to extend 6 inches beyond the outer walls of the base. Unless the soil is very unstable, you can pour the footing in the excavation without building a wooden form for it; but if you dig a deep pit, you may have to shore the walls.

The first construction step is to lay out both the outdoor base area and the sections that are to be cut away from the house wall and the floor. Follow the instructions on the opposite page to draw outlines on the wall and the floor. Then you are ready to lay out the excavation site with stakes and string.

In constructing the base, build everything up to slab level before you cut more than a small opening in the house wall. That way, you will lessen the amount of time your house is left open to dirt, bugs and other people's pets. Pour the concrete footing first, then use the techniques described on pages 72 and 73 to build up the block-and-brick walls. To keep the walls plumb, level and straight, have on hand a mason's level, a mason's line and a story pole—the latter is a special mason's ruler used to measure the height of courses of brick and block.

Since the fireplace base is rectangular, you must begin laying the courses at a corner, with what is called a corner lead. The block corner lead used in the following construction is two courses high and consists of three blocks; the first two are laid perpendicular to each other at the corner, and the third is laid atop the first two, covering the joint between them. The three-course brick corner lead consists of six bricks laid in the pattern shown in Step 3, page 80, to form a wall two bricks thick. Lay dry runs of each course before you add mortar, to determine how many blocks or bricks you must break (page 74) for an exact fit. Since block can be difficult to break, you may prefer to substitute 12-inch blocks for some of the usual 16-inch blocks.

Incorporated into this masonry base are an ashpit to collect waste from the firebox above and an air inlet to feed outside air up through an opening in the firebox floor. The ashpit, a hollow area inside the base, has one opening into the firebox floor and one at the back wall of the base; the pit can be any size and has no special placement requirements.

However, the placement of the air inlet in a fireplace that is added to an existing house is complicated. The vent to the outside can be located anywhere on the outer base walls, but for the inlet to work efficiently, the opening into the firebox must be located at the front and center of the firebox floor. In addition, the inlet must measure 55 square inches or more

in cross section at all points. Fulfilling these specifications requires careful planning when the fireplace base abuts the house foundation, for air must flow up over part of the base wall, then over the house foundation as well. The inlet design on these pages provides all of the required clearances.

You will need two metal fittings to finish the ashpit area: a 4½-by-9-inch pivoting cover, the ash-dump door, for the firebox floor; and a 12-by-12-inch door for the outside wall of the ashpit. For the air inlet you will need an inlet damper the size of one firebrick, 4½ by 13 inches, and a vent for the outside wall. All of these fittings are available through stores carrying fireplace or masonry hardware. If your vent opening is an odd size, you can make a screen vent from fine wire mesh.

When the base reaches slab level, you must cut through the house wall and the floor, then frame the openings. The illustrations on the following pages show the techniques for opening a bearing wall in which the joists run perpendicular to the wall. But the instructions accompanying the pictures also include alternate methods for working with joists that run parallel to the wall.

The hearth slab is the final step in the construction of the fireplace base. Made of reinforced concrete 4 to 6 inches thick (depending on local building codes), the slab rests on the base outside the house and is cantilevered into the house to fill the floor opening. The slab on these pages is poured to a depth designed to accept a hearth finished with brick; if the finished hearth will be tile, marble, slate or another material thinner than brick, you will have to adjust the height of the slab under the hearth by adding to the slab thickness there.

A second type of hearth—one that is suspended, shelflike, above the floor—requires special cutting and forming techniques. The opening in the house wall is cut and framed like that for a window, and no opening is cut in the floor. Instead, a boxlike form is constructed 12 inches above floor level, and propped up with shoring until the concrete poured into the form hardens. The thickness of this raised slab also depends on the hearth finish material.

Laying Out and Framing the House-Wall Openings

Before you cut through a wall and a floor to install a fireplace, you must consider the effect of those openings on the framework of the house. Almost certainly you will need to reinforce the existing wall and floor with new studs, joists and doubled headers.

The placement of these various reinforcing elements will depend on the exact location of the openings in relation to the existing structural members—and to locate those members you will have to open a portion of the wall. But the placement of new joists and studs will also be dictated by building codes, which generally stipulate that there must be 2 inches of clearance between any combustible framing materials and the brickwork of a firebox. This means that in some instances you must not only reinforce the existing structure but remove a joist or stud that lies too close to the opening.

Before cutting away a portion of the wall, mark the dimensions of the firebox opening *(chart, page 70)* on the interior house wall. Add an extra 16 inches on each side of the firebox for the brick jambs and an extra 28 inches above the firebox for the chimney breast *(cross section, page 71)*. Drill through to the exterior wall at the four corners of the plotted opening and, using a mason's level, connect the holes with a chalk line, outlining the opening.

Having marked the wall opening, then mark the floor opening. Snap a chalk line across the floor at each edge of the wall opening, perpendicular to the wall. Measure out 16 inches along each line, and drill holes through the floor and subfloor, marking the outer corners of the hearth. Finally, from the outside, cut away an 18-inch-wide swath of siding and sheathing along the bottom edge of the plotted wall opening, using a circular saw. This will disclose the pattern of studs and joists in the affected area.

To calculate the structural changes needed to frame the wall opening, first determine the position of the jack studs that will support the doubled header. If an existing king stud is less than 3½ inches from the edge of the opening,

you will have to remove it and install a new king stud 3½ inches away, then nail a jack stud to it. If an existing king stud is more than 3½ inches but less than 6 inches from the edge of the opening, nail one or two jack studs to it—to bring the frame the requisite 2 inches from the edge of the opening. If the existing king stud is more than 6 inches from the opening, simply install a new stud, 3½ inches away from the opening, and add the jack stud as above.

The placement of new framing members for the floor opening will depend on whether the existing joists run parallel or perpendicular to the wall opening. If they run parallel, you probably will need to cut only the joist closest to the wall. A new doubled joist should be installed, flush with the front edge of the floor opening, and two doubled headers should frame the sides of the floor opening. In addition, this framing will serve as the form

for the poured-concrete hearth slab.

If the joists run perpendicular to the wall opening, you will need to cut a number of old joists and add new joists. If the nearest joist on a side is less than 3 inches from the edge of the opening, you will have to remove that joist and add a new doubled joist, framing the edge of the opening. If the nearest joist is more than 3 inches but less than 8 inches from the opening, you can double it and then add a single new joist, at the edge of the opening. If the nearest joist is more than 8 inches from the opening, simply add a new doubled joist at the edge of the opening. A doubled header, spanning the front edge of the opening, will be nailed to the framing joists.

Locating the framing members. Within each opening in the wall and floor, the studs and joists must be cut away, and the bordering framing members must be reinforced.

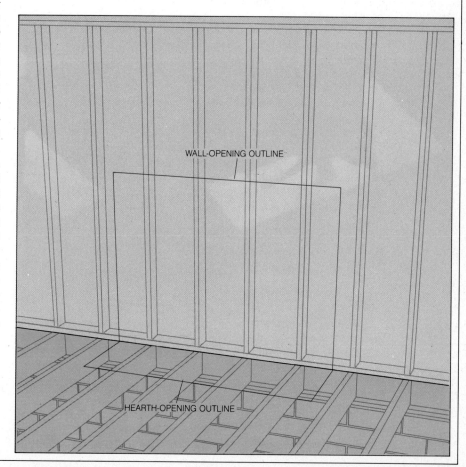

WALL-OPENING OUTLINE

HEARTH-OPENING OUTLINE

Building the Base with Block and Brick

1 Laying out the site. To outline the excavation pit for the fireplace base and its concrete footing, first mark the siding 6 inches out from each side of the wall opening *(right)*. At each mark, use a level to draw a plumb line on the house foundation. About 8 inches up from the ground on each line, drive a masonry nail into a mortar joint, and tie a string to the nail. Then hold the short leg of a framing square against the foundation, with the corner of the square against the nail, and have a helper extend a string along the long leg of the square. At a point 8 inches beyond the planned length of the side of the footing *(page 70),* have a helper fasten the string to a stake and pound the stake into the ground.

Establish a line for the opposite side in the same way. Then, measuring out from the foundation along each line, tie a string to mark the planned length of the side of the footing *(inset)* Stretch a third string across two of these marks, extending it 8 inches past the side strings.

To check that the corners are square, measure the diagonal distances from corner to corner; adjust the stakes, if necessary, until the distances are equal. Then excavate to the planned depth of the base plus the depth of the footing, digging 4 inches below a mortar joint in the house foundation. Remove all strings and stakes.

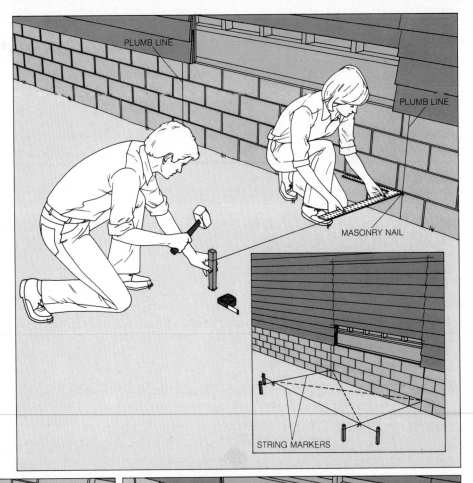

PLUMB LINE

PLUMB LINE

MASONRY NAIL

STRING MARKERS

2 Installing and leveling grade pegs. Near each corner of the pit and at the center, drive a 16-inch length of ½-inch reinforcing rod (rebar) 4 inches into the ground. Lay a level on edge across adjacent pegs, and adjust the pegs until all of the tops are level. Measure to be sure that each peg protrudes at least 1 foot above the ground; scoop up dirt from around the bottom of a peg, if necessary, until 1 foot of the peg is exposed. Then smooth and level the bottom of the pit, tamping the dirt firmly around each peg.

3 Positioning the reinforcing rods. Cut pieces of ½-inch rebar to fit the length and width of the pit; lay them, supported on brick pieces, at 8-inch intervals across the bottom of the pit to form a steel grid. Wire the rods together where they intersect, and wire the rods to the grade pegs.

Pour in concrete *(page 72)* to the tops of the grade pegs. Smooth and level the concrete with a wood float. Allow the footing to cure for 24 hours before proceeding.

At the Bottom, a Concrete Footing

1 Outlining the base on the footing. Use the technique illustrated in Step 1, opposite, to reconstruct a string outline the exact length and width of the planned base. Then drop a plumb bob to the footing at the two outer corners of the outline, and have a helper mark the corners on the concrete. To mark the inside corners, use a level to draw plumb lines down the house foundation, from the edges of the wall opening to the footing. Snap three chalk lines across the concrete to connect the corners.

PLUMB LINE

FUTURE PLUMB LINE

MASON'S LINE

FACE COURSE

STORY POLE

TWO-COURSE CORNER

CORNER BLOCK

.MASON'S LEVEL

2 Laying the first block course. Using semisolid concrete blocks—those with thick walls and small holes—lay a corner lead two blocks high at each of the four corners of the base outline. To begin each lead, spread a 1½-inch-thick mortar bed for the first block and set the block in place; tap it down with the handle of a trowel until the mortar is ⅜ inch thick and the top of the block is level with the first 8-inch mark on a mason's story pole. Lay the second block in the same manner, buttering the end with mortar where it adjoins the first block; then lay the third block atop the first two, aligning its top with the second 8-inch mark on the story pole. Use a mason's level to be sure that each corner is level, plumb and straight.

Fasten a mason's line to the two outside corner leads at the level of the first mortar joint *(inset)*, and lay a row of blocks between the leads, aligning the outside faces of the blocks with the mason's line. Then lay the parallel row of blocks against the house foundation, again using a mason's level to keep the block faces flush. To complete the first course, lay blocks between the front and back corners, along each side. Finally, fill in the central core, breaking blocks to fit if necessary. Mortar the core blocks in place, checking to be sure their tops are level. Lay succeeding courses of blocks in the same way, filling in the central core as you go. Stop about 8 inches below ground level.

3 **Laying the first brick courses.** Build a wall two bricks thick around the edge of the concrete-block base. Begin by laying a corner lead three courses high at each outer corner of the base, using galvanized-steel masonry ties to link the front and back bricks in each course and metal mesh to cover the top of the concrete block. Rest the end of a mason's level on the footing, and check to be sure that the two faces of each corner lead are level, plumb and straight.

Fill in the three courses of bricks established by the corner leads, working all around the base. Then fill in the core with a layer of mortared concrete blocks, cutting the blocks where necessary for fit and making sure their tops are level. Finally, lay one more double course of bricks around the perimeter of the base, and fill in the pit around the base to ground level (inset).

4 **Starting the air inlet and the ashpit.** To locate the center of the planned air inlet, find the midpoint between the two sides of the wall opening, and mark points 6½ inches on both sides of this midpoint. From each mark, draw a plumb line on the house foundation down to the brick wall; extend the line across the top of the bricks. Establish two partition walls in the base by laying a row of bricks end to end across the base at each guideline, leaving at least 7 inches of space between the two rows. Pave the floor of the ashpit with a layer of mortared bricks, laid flat.

BACK COURSE

FACE COURSE

MASONRY TIE

THREE-COURSE CORNER LEAD

AIR INLET

ASHPIT

5 **Framing openings in the base.** Continue raising the four sides of the base and the partition walls. For the ashpit door, leave a 1-foot-wide gap beginning one brick course above ground level; for the air-inlet vent, leave a gap as wide as the passageway between the two partitions, starting three brick courses above ground level.

When the height of the ashpit opening reaches 12 inches, install lintels across the tops of both openings. For each lintel, have two 3-by-3½-inch angle irons cut 6 inches longer than the opening they will bridge. Hold the 3½-inch legs of each pair of irons back to back, and press the horizontal legs into a mortar bed laid atop the bricks on either side of the opening; align the joint between the vertical legs with the joint between the double wall of bricks. Continue raising the brick walls and partitions until they are level with the bottom of the last course of blocks in the house foundation; mortar bricks directly to the horizontal legs of the lintels. Mortar the ashpit door and the air-inlet vent into place, adding extra mortar to fill any gaps around the edges.

AIR INLET

ASHPIT

LINTELS

6 **Finishing the base.** Build up the outer brick walls and partitions three courses, until they are level with the top of the last course of blocks in the house foundation. Then, as you build up the wall against the house, leave an opening between the guidelines that mark the air-inlet partitions *(inset)*.

With cavities for the air inlet and the ashpit established, fill in the third hollow section of the base—in this example, the area to the left of the air inlet—with mortared blocks or mortar and rubble. Place a sheet of ½-inch plywood over the entire base to protect the masonry and to create a surface for you to stand on.

SPACE TO BE FILLED

RUBBLE

AIR INLET

ASHPIT DOOR

PARTITION WALLS

Cutting Through the House Wall and Floor

1 **Reinforcing the floor joists.** Working below the house floor, locate the pilot holes that define the planned hearth; measure the distance to the nearest joist on each side. Reinforce or replace these joists *(page 77)*. To double an existing joist or create a new doubled joist, nail two lengths of lumber together with 16-penny (3½-inch) nails; put three nails at each end and stagger nails at 12-inch intervals.

Wedge a 4-by-4 support post under each joist between the doubled joists, 18 inches beyond the front of the planned hearth. Then cut out the joists within the hearth area; make one cut flush with the house band joist at the foundation wall and a second cut 3 inches beyond the front of the planned hearth.

If the joists run parallel to the wall opening, cut away a section of the joist that is closest to the wall; the length of the cut section should equal the planned width of the hearth, plus 3 inches on each side. Then install a new doubled joist the required distance from the front edge of the firebox, as described on page 77. (For a firebox whose front edge is going to be flush with the inside surface of the house wall, you must measure in from the house wall to establish a position for the new doubled joist.)

HEARTH POSITION

BAND JOIST

ADDED JOIST

EXISTING JOIST

2 **Installing a doubled header.** Assemble a doubled header to fit between the doubled joists, and
fasten 3-inch joist hangers to both ends of the
new header. Have a helper hold the header in position, butted against the ends of the cut
joists; nail the joist hangers to the doubled joists.
Then fasten 1½-inch joist hangers to the
cut joists, and nail the hangers to the header.

If the joists run parallel to the wall, install a doubled header along each side of the planned
hearth opening. Using 90° framing connectors,
fasten one end of each doubled header to the
band joist at the house wall, and the other end to
the doubled joist that you have installed beyond the front of the hearth. Then nail joist hangers to each doubled header, to hold the ends
of the cut joist that it intersects.

DOUBLED JOIST

JOIST HANGER

BAND JOIST

DOUBLED HEADER

DOUBLED JOIST

3 **Building a shoring wall.** Assemble and erect
a floor-to-ceiling framework of 2-by-4s in front of
the opening outline on the interior wall. For
the framework, cut a sole plate and a top plate at
least 1 foot longer than the opening, and mark
the plates at 24-inch intervals for studs. Then cut
the studs, making them 4½ inches shorter
than the distance from floor to ceiling. Lay the top
plate and the sole plate on edge on the floor,
a stud's length apart, with the stud marks facing
each other. Position the studs at the marks,
and nail the plates to the studs. Brace the framework with two diagonal 2-by-4s nailed across

the studs, one on each side. Staple strips of ¼-
inch-thick padding to the upper surface of the
top plate, to protect the ceiling.

Cut a strip of ¼-inch plywood 4 inches wide and
slightly longer than the shoring wall. Position
the strip about 4 feet from the house wall, centered in front of the opening and, with a helper, lift the shoring wall onto the strip. While your
helper holds the shoring wall plumb, tap shims
between the plywood strip and the sole plate at
each stud, working from both sides, until the
shoring wall presses firmly against the ceiling.

4 **Cutting through the exterior wall.** Standing
on top of the plywood-covered base outside the
house, cut along the outline of the opening
(page 77), using a carbide-tipped circular-saw
blade set to the depth of the siding. Pry the
siding away from the sheathing behind it. Then
set the blade of the saw deep enough to cut
through the sheathing; cut and pry the sheathing away from the studs.

5 **Cutting the studs.** Working inside the house, cut away a floor-to-ceiling section of wall covering over the area of the opening, going as far as the first studs that are more than 3 inches past the sides of the opening. Pull away any insulation over the area of the opening, then mark and cut each stud 11½ inches above the top of the opening. Pull and twist the studs away from the sole plate; then cut through the sole plate at the sides of the opening, and pry up the plate.

6 **Installing jack studs.** On each side of the opening, install one or more jack studs the height of the opening plus 2 inches, positioning them as described on page 77. Nail them to the king studs with 12-penny (3¼-inch) nails, spaced 4 to 6 inches apart. Be sure to leave the necessary 2-inch clearance between the outer jack studs and the edges of the opening.

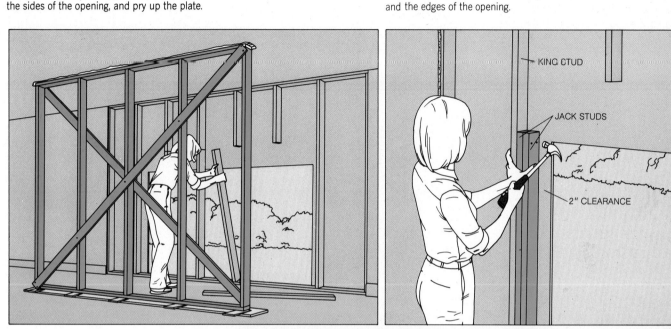

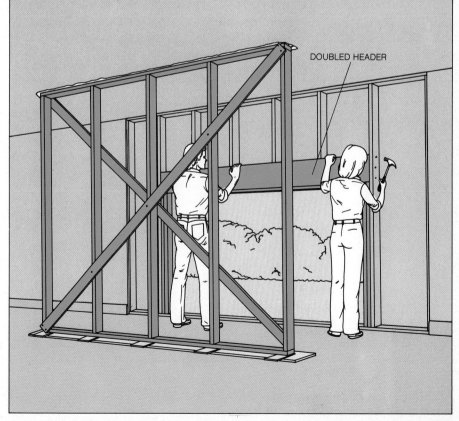

7 **Installing the header.** Assemble a doubled header of ½-inch plywood between two 2-by-10s, measured and cut to fit between the inside faces of the king studs. Fasten the header assembly together with 16-penny nails, staggered at 10-inch intervals. With a helper, set the header atop the jack studs and nail it to the king studs; toenail it to the jack studs. Finally, toenail the cripple studs above the opening to the top of the header. Then take down the shoring wall.

8 **Cutting through the floor.** Cut through the finish floor and the subfloor along the hearth outline *(page 77)*; use a saber saw to begin the cut in the corner pilot holes, then switch to a circular saw when the cuts are long enough. Pry up the floor and the subfloor.

Cut the finish floor back another 2 inches around the three outer edges of the hearth area, leaving the subfloor intact. This area will be trimmed with a frame of corner-mitered hardwood strips when the hearth is finished *(page 111)*.

9 **Removing the band joist and the sill.** Remove the plywood cover from the fireplace base. With a crosscut saw, cut through the outer band joist flush with the edges of the opening; knock out the cut section. Then cut through the sill that rests on top of the foundation, cutting on both sides of each anchor bolt within the opening; remove the sill in sections. Use a pry bar to dig out the pieces of wood trapped under the bolts; then use a hacksaw to cut the bolts off flush with the top of the house foundation.

SILL

ANCHOR BOLT

Preparations for the Hearth Slab

1 Bringing the brickwork to floor level. Lay two courses of bricks across the top of the house foundation, leaving a space between the inner faces of the two partition walls, which form the air inlet. On each course, set the bricks long sides together, ends out, in what is commonly called a header course. Wall off half of the space left for the air inlet by laying two courses of brick lengthwise, across the inner face of the house foundation, creating a one-brick-deep indentation along the outer face of the foundation.

Lay two more double-width courses of bricks around the perimeter of the base, to bring the brickwork level with the top of the header courses. Add rubble to the solid core section, to bring it level with the brickwork. Then complete the base by laying three single-width courses of bricks around the three outer walls, creating a lip for the sheet-metal cover that will underlay the hearth slab. Begin these courses with 3-course corner leads at the two outside corners; work in along the sides of the base, cutting the last bricks as needed to line up with the house wall (*inset*). Check the top of each corner lead with a mason's level to be sure it is level with the surface of the inside floor. Continue to check this level as you work, adjusting the mortar thickness, if necessary, so that the top of each section of the wall lies exactly at floor level.

Cut a template of ¼-inch plywood for the sheet-metal cover. Make it large enough to butt against the three single-width walls that form the lip, and to overlap the house foundation to the midpoint of the just-laid header course.

2 Marking the plywood template. Draw lines on top of the plywood template to establish the location of the inner walls and the front edge of the planned firebox (*page 71*). Cut the plywood to fit in the firebox space. Mark both edges of the two partition walls. Position the ash-dump door inside the firebox outline, as far toward the rear of the firebox as possible. Outline the vertical flange of the door on the plywood. Notch the edge of the plywood where it covers the gap in the header course left for the air inlet; make the notch 13 inches long and 4½ inches deep.

Have a sheet-metal fabricator cut a piece of 10-gauge sheet metal the same size as the template, piercing it with a hole for the ash-dump door and with a notch for the air inlet. Then set the sheet-metal cover in place over the base.

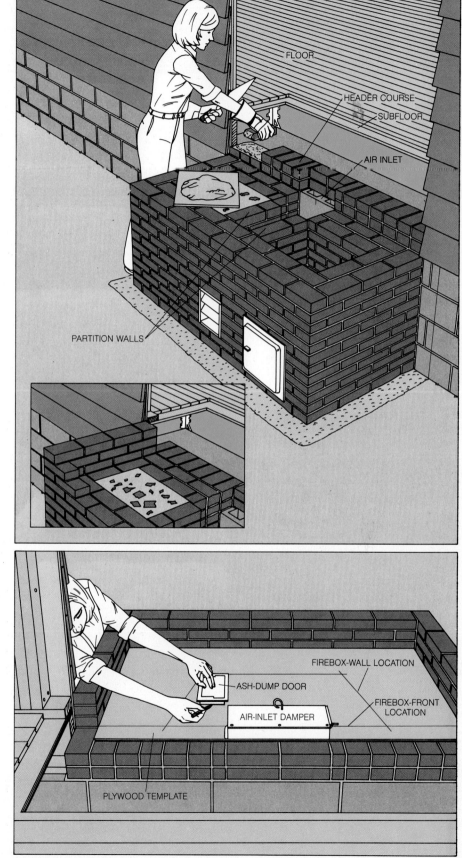

FLOOR

HEADER COURSE

SUBFLOOR

AIR INLET

PARTITION WALLS

FIREBOX-WALL LOCATION

ASH-DUMP DOOR

AIR-INLET DAMPER

FIREBOX-FRONT LOCATION

PLYWOOD TEMPLATE

3 **Forming the slab openings.** Construct 8-inch-high box forms from ½-inch plywood to fit over the ash-dump hole and the air-inlet notch in the sheet-metal cover. Construct each box so that its inside dimensions match exactly the dimensions of the opening in the sheet metal, and join the pieces with continuous butt joints. Then nail a 1-by-1-inch strip, 6 inches long, to each inside face of each box so that the strips extend 2 to 3 inches past the bottom edges *(inset)*. The strips will brace the box forms so that they do not shift position when the concrete is poured; the continuous butt joints will make the forms easy to disassemble after the concrete has hardened. Position the boxes over the holes, and grease their outside surfaces with motor oil.

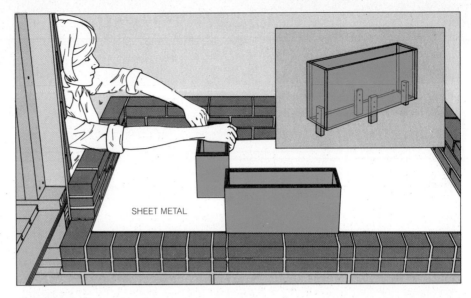

SHEET METAL

Pouring the Concrete Hearth

1 **Installing the form boards.** If the sides of the hearth opening are not framed by doubled joists installed as in Step 1, page 81, cut two form boards to fit between the doubled header joist and the band joist. Nail 90° framing connectors to the ends of each side board, facing the opening. Align the boards' inside faces with the edge of the opening; nail the connectors to the doubled header. Wedge scrap lumber between the form board and the doubled joist, on top of the sill; toenail the form board to it.

To support the floor of the form, nail 2-by-2-inch ledger strips to the form boards and the doubled header *(inset)*. Cut the strips about 8 inches shorter than the boards and align the top of the strips with the top of the brick header course.

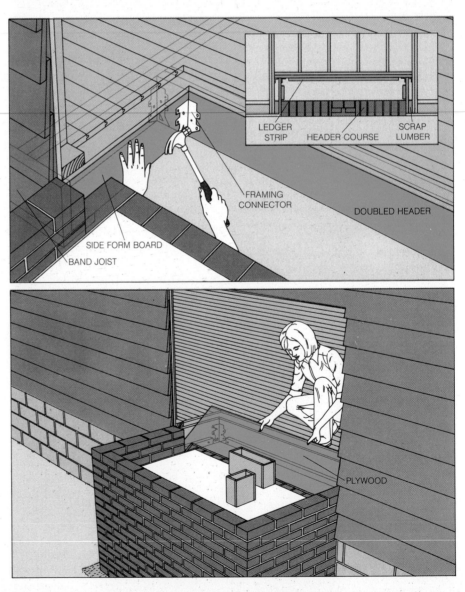

LEDGER STRIP   HEADER COURSE   SCRAP LUMBER

FRAMING CONNECTOR

DOUBLED HEADER

SIDE FORM BOARD

BAND JOIST

PLYWOOD

2 **Making a floor for the form.** Measure and cut a piece of ½-inch plywood for the floor of the hearth form. Cut the plywood to butt against the form boards and the doubled header; on the fourth edge, cut two small ears, so that the plywood will butt against the sheet-metal edge and wrap around the corners of the sheet metal to abut the brickwork of the base. Set the floor in place, its edges resting on the brick header course and on the ledger strips. Support the plywood from beneath with 4-by-4 posts, one at each corner and two in the center.

3 **Positioning the reinforcing rods.** Lay lengths of ½-inch reinforcing rod (rebar) at 8-inch intervals, crisscrossing the hearth and firebox. Support the rebar 2 inches above the plywood and the sheet metal with brick fragments, and fasten the rods together at the intersections with wire.

Pour the concrete slab so that its surface is level with the bottom of the top mortar joint in the back wall of the base, leaving one brick course extending above the concrete.

4 **Leveling the concrete.** Smooth and level the concrete with a wood float, taking care not to jostle the box forms framing the openings for the air inlet and the ashpit. Allow the concrete to set for six to seven days, then knock out the box forms and remove the 4-by-4 supports.

A Hearth Suspended above the Floor

A frame and a form for a cantilevered slab. The exterior masonry base for a raised hearth is constructed in the same way as the base shown on pages 78-81, but the brickwork rises 12 inches above floor level. The wall opening is framed with king and jack studs at the sides, a doubled header and cripple studs above, a 2-by-4 sill supported by cripple studs below (inset). The jack studs are 2 inches back from the sides of the opening; the bottom of the header is 28 inches above the planned top of the firebox (page 70); and the top of the sill is 12 inches above the floor. The sheathing and siding are cut back

6 inches from each side of the opening, to make room for the slab form.

The three-sided box form for the slab is made of three 2-by-8s and has a ½-inch plywood floor. The sides of the box extend 20 inches into the room beyond the inner wall surface, and they are nailed into the side walls of the masonry base 12 inches beyond the exterior wall surface. One edge of the plywood floor butts against the front edge of the masonry base, level with the sill; the other edges are nailed to the bottom edges of the 2-by-8s. The entire form is supported by

two shoring walls made of 9-inch-high studs nailed at 16-inch intervals between top and sole plates. Two 1-by-3s nailed across the top of the box, 4 inches from the ends of the side boards, provide extra bracing. Scraps of ½-inch plywood wedged between the side boards and the jack studs temporarily fill the gaps left by the required 2-inch clearance.

The box is greased inside as in Step 3, opposite. The concrete slab is reinforced and poured as in Step 3, above. After it has set, the shoring walls and the entire box form are removed.

Erecting the Firebox and Smoke Chamber

The plain masonry jacket of a modern fireplace hides an array of precisely ordered slopes, ledges and spaces whose careful placement determines the efficiency—and longevity—of the fireplace.

The firebox, smoke shelf and smoke chamber, though distinct from their surrounding exterior masonry, are built with it, almost course by course, as a unit. Each course—whether it is of standard brick or of firebrick—is laid without mortar first, in a trial run called dry bonding. This technique makes it possible for you to adjust mortar-joint widths and to cut bricks to the exact sizes that will ensure a strong and symmetrical course before you cement the bricks permanently in place. Dry bonding is especially important in building the slope of the fireback, where the corner bricks must be cut at compound angles.

To make the smoke chamber slope inward from the damper to the flue, a bricklaying technique called corbeling is used. In corbeling, each course of bricks is offset up to 1 inch over the edge of the course below it, creating a stepped effect. A corbeled smoke chamber is sturdier and less likely to leak if it is two courses thick. Strengthen such a double corbeled wall by laying an occasional brick perpendicular to the bricks below.

The back of the firebox and the inside of the smoke chamber are covered with a layer of mortar ¼ to ½ inch thick—a coating known to masons as parging. On the firebox, parging serves to seal and insulate the structure; in the smoke chamber, it smooths the path of smoke rising past the corbeled bricks. Parge the firebox with special fireplace mortar and the smoke chamber with regular masonry mortar. Mortar for parging should be slightly drier than normal so that it will stick to the bricks better; even so, a good deal of mortar will fall off. On corbeled bricks, apply the mortar in two coats, one to fill in the stepped offsets, the other to build up a smooth surface.

For strength and to prevent cracks and leaks, the space between the outer walls and the firebox and smoke chamber must be filled in solidly with rubble. Use whole bricks and concrete blocks for large spaces, broken bits of masonry for tight corners. Stabilize this rubble with plenty of mortar; tie it to adjacent walls with galvanized-steel masonry ties, set crosswise and embedded in the mortar joints of the rubble and the walls.

Getting the Firebox Under Way

ASH DUMP

AIR INLET

JAMB

JAMB

1 **Laying the firebox floor.** Lay a dry run of firebricks over the concrete slab, working from the firebox front to the back. To mark the firebox front, snap a chalk line between the two inside edges of the wall opening. Then lay two standard bricks end to end at each side of the opening and flush with the chalk line; these bricks will be the first course of the fireplace jambs. Mortar the jamb bricks to the slab and to the exterior masonry wall of the fireplace base.

Allowing spaces ⅛ inch wide for mortar joints, add as many firebricks as will fit between the jamb bricks and the sides of the air-inlet hole. Center a second row of firebricks behind the first row, extending the ends of this row a half-brick beyond the inside ends of the fireplace jambs. Continue laying firebrick rows of this width to within 1 or 2 inches of the back edge of the concrete slab. Cut bricks as necessary to fit around the ash-dump opening.

When you are satisfied with the arrangement and spacing of the firebricks, remove them from the slab in sequence. Spread a ½-inch bed of special fireplace mortar on the floor area, and lay the firebricks permanently in place with ⅛-inch mortar joints between them.

Check each row with a level; tamp down bricks that protrude. Insert the air-inlet damper and ash-dump door in their openings (inset).

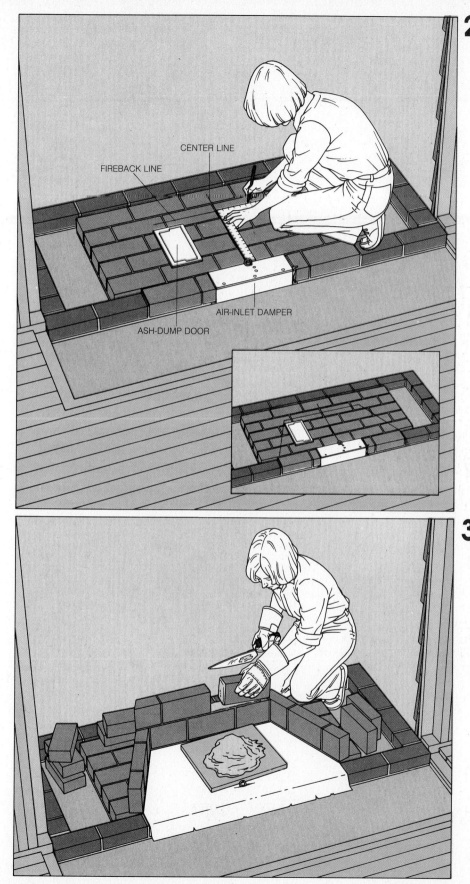

CENTER LINE

FIREBACK LINE

AIR-INLET DAMPER

ASH-DUMP DOOR

2 **Establishing the firebox walls.** Mark a center line on the firebox floor midway between the side walls of the slab. Then, using the dimensions in the chart on page 70, measure from the back edge of the air-inlet damper and mark the center line at the desired depth of the fireback. From this mark, use a carpenter's square to run perpendicular lines, half the width of the fireback, on each side of the center line. Use a straight-edge to connect the ends of the fireback line to the inside back corners of the inner bricks at the end of each jamb (inset).

3 **Laying the vertical wall sections.** Build up the first three courses of the firebox walls (the vertical portion of most firebacks is 14 inches high— about three firebricks). Position the wide faces of the firebricks vertically and align them with the firebox outline. Allow for ¼-inch joints, and lay the front brick on each side wall snug against the corner of the jamb. At the back corners of the firebox, cut the end bricks at angles so that they butt against each other and join in a continuous running-bond pattern. When you mortar the bricks in place, check the top and the face of each course with a level. Cover the floor of the firebox with heavy paper, a plastic sheet or a layer of sand to catch any mortar spills.

4 **Parging the firebox.** Coat the outside surfaces of the first three courses of the firebox with a layer of special fireplace mortar ¼ inch thick, to seal the bricks completely. Using a mason's trowel, spread the mortar from the bottom up. As you build the walls of the firebox, stop every few courses to parge the outside.

Building the Walls That Form the Firebox

1 **Building the masonry liner.** Lay a course of standard bricks around the back and sides of the firebox. Set the corners of the two end bricks against the backs of the jambs and, if necessary, mortar extra firebricks to the slab to support these end bricks. Leave an expansion gap ½ to 1 inch wide between this masonry liner and the parged walls of the firebox; the back wall of the masonry liner should be located almost flush with the exterior wall of the fireplace. Build up the masonry liner, the exterior walls and the fireplace jambs to the same height as the vertical section of the firebox.

2 **Filling the hollows with rubble.** Using plenty of mortar, pack the cavities between the masonry liner and the exterior walls with fragments of brick and concrete block. Use whole bricks or blocks to fill the larger spaces. Lay the rubble randomly any way that it fits, filling in with mortar. Straight courses and uniform joints are not necessary, but do not leave any spaces unfilled.

An Inward Slope for the Fireback

1 Making a pattern. Measure the height of the vertical fireback you constructed in Step 3, page 89, and draw a line this length along one side of a sheet of ¼-inch plywood. Then measure the width of the damper you are going to install, from the outside edge of the front flange to the inside edge of the rear flange (*left inset, below*). Subtract this measurement from the planned depth of your firebox floor (*page 70, chart*), and use a carpenter's square to draw a line of this length, forming a right angle with one end of the first line. Perpendicular to the end of this second line, draw a third line parallel to the first line, making it the same length as the planned firebox height (*page 70, chart*). Connect the end of this third line to the free end of the first line; this last line will mark the slope required for the fireback (*right inset, below*).

Cut along the lines marking the slope and floor of the firebox. Then measure 3 inches out from the line marking the firebox height, and cut the fourth side of the pattern; this extra width will make the pattern sturdier and easier to use.

2 Completing the firebox walls. Use the plywood pattern to establish the angle of the firebricks above the vertical fireback. To set the first brick, put a thick line of mortar along the center portion of the fireback. Set a firebrick in the mortar, centering it over a vertical mortar joint and tipping it forward until its face rests against the sloped edge of the plywood. The mortar joint should be ¼ inch thick in front, widening to a wedge at the back. Steady the brick for several seconds to let the mortar bond. Move the plywood and set the adjacent bricks.

As you raise the sloping fireback, continue to raise the side walls as well, cutting the corner bricks of the side walls to fit both the slope of the fireback and the angle of the side walls (*inset*). Because of the forward slope, you will be unable to maintain the running-bond pattern at the corners above the first course of the sloping fireback—the horizontal joints of the fireback will then fall below those of the side walls. The end bricks in each course of the sloping fireback must lean on the end bricks of the side walls.

Raise the walls to their full height, parging the outside every few courses as you go. When you reach the top, run an extra-thick layer of mortar across the top of the sloping fireback, to bring it up to the level of the side walls.

Sculpting a Smoke Shelf That Works

1 **Building up to the smoke shelf.** Raise the masonry liner behind the firebox, the exterior walls, the jambs around the fireplace opening, and the rubble fill inside the exterior walls. Corbel the back of the masonry liner to follow the slope of the fireback, but leave about an inch of expansion space between them. To support and counterweight the corbeled bricks, fill the space behind each course with mortared rubble. As soon as the space between the corbeled liner and the exterior rear wall is wide enough to accommodate a full brick, resume building a double thickness of brick up the rear wall.

Raise the inner masonry liner to within 2 or 3 inches of the top of the firebox. Then, when you are laying the final course, set the bricks perpendicular to the firebox walls, thus sealing off the narrow air space between the firebox and the liner. Be sure this final course is snugly mortared against the firebox.

Raise the doubled rear wall one course above the height of the firebox, but build up the jambs only to the planned height of the fireplace opening. Build up the exterior side walls only partially, so that the sides step down from the exterior rear wall to the top of the jamb. The steps will allow you to interlock the bricks of the side walls with the bricks of the chimney breast.

2 **Parging the smoke shelf.** Spread a layer of masonry mortar ¼ to ½ inch thick between the top of the fireback and the exterior rear wall. To make an effective smoke shelf, trowel the mortar into a smooth, slightly concave surface that covers the top course of the masonry liner and curves up against the exterior wall.

Build up rubble behind the jambs and the stepped-down exterior side walls until it is level with the bricks around the smoke shelf. Together with the top of the masonry liner, the rubble will support the lintel over the fireplace opening.

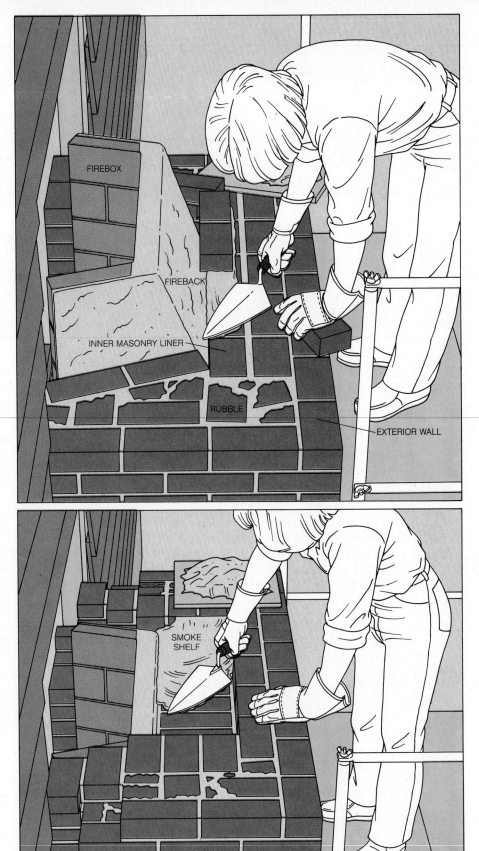

Where to Set the Damper and Lintels

1 **Installing the damper.** Set the damper on top of the firebox, with its hinged plate to the rear and its front flange flush with the front edges of the firebox walls. Be sure the back flange rests securely on the top edge of the fireback—if it does not, adjust the damper position slightly. Lift each end of the damper, and wrap the side flange with fiberglass insulation; this will allow the metal to expand without cracking the masonry. Open the damper plate from time to time while you build the smoke chamber, to be sure the plate clears the inner masonry walls.

2 **Setting the lintels.** Lay two angle irons, ¼ inch by 3 inches, across the fireplace front, one to support the corbeled bricks above the damper, the other to support the bricks that span the fireplace opening. Position the front angle iron across the tops of the jambs, overlapping them 4 to 6 inches at each end; set the vertical face of the angle iron flush against the front corners of the firebox walls. Wrap fiberglass insulation over the ends of the angle iron. Set the rear angle iron on the masonry one course higher than the front flange of the damper. Line up the vertical face of this angle iron with the front corners of the firebox wall. The other face should almost touch the dome of the damper. Wrap fiberglass over the ends.

3 **Raising the chimney breast.** Lay a course of bricks across the lintel over the fireplace opening, mortaring the end bricks to the stepped-down bricks of the exterior side wall. As you lay additional courses across the chimney breast, alternately overlap the end bricks of the breast and the exterior wall, creating a continuous running-bond pattern that wraps the front corners of the fireplace. Rather than completing the side walls, step down the bricks as you did in Step 1, opposite, but this time toward the back wall.

Raise the chimney breast to within 2 inches of the header at the top of the wall opening. When you are laying the last few courses, you will have to work alternately inside and outside the house to bring the walls together.

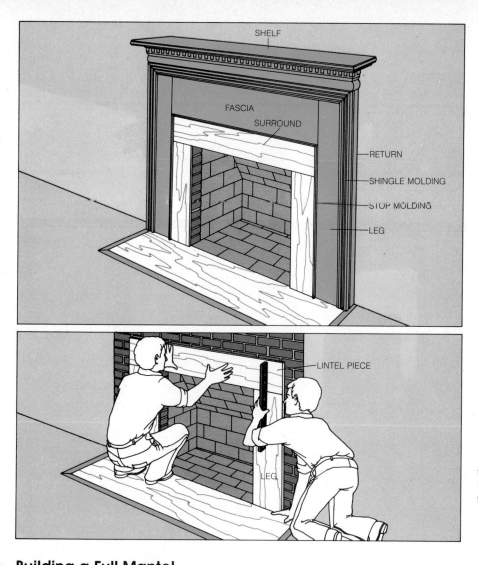

SHELF

FASCIA

SURROUND

RETURN

SHINGLE MOLDING

STOP MOLDING

LEG

LINTEL PIECE

LEG

The Ultimate Adornment: A Full Mantel

Anatomy of the finished mantel. The full mantel, installed with a marble surround framing the fireplace opening, consists of a plywood frame with a crosspiece fascia board at the top and two side pieces called legs. A mantel shelf, constructed of molding in a fashion similar to the one opposite, has been attached to the frame. Underneath the shelf, fluted shingle molding runs across the top of the fascia and down the sides of the legs. Stop molding is fitted to the frame's inner edge and allows the mantel to overlap the surround, concealing the brick facing. The frame is held away from the wall by two side pieces called returns, which compensate for the contours of the wall surfaces. To secure the mantel to the wall, the returns are toenailed to the studs flanking the fireplace and to a cleat attached to the chimney breast *(Step 3, opposite)*.

Installing a marble surround. Spread thin-set cement over the area of the brick facing to be covered by the surround. Then, with the aid of a helper, lift the side pieces of the surround into place and press them against the cement until cement oozes out at the edges. Plumb the side pieces with a mason's level, then lift the lintel into place, resting it on top of the side pieces. Plumb the lintel to align it with the side pieces. Then trowel and smooth cement into the gaps between the surround and the brick edge of the firebox. Allow the cement to cure for 24 hours before you install the full mantel.

Building a Full Mantel

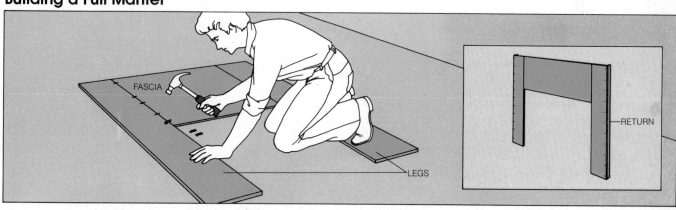

FASCIA

LEGS

RETURN

1 Making the frame. Cut two sections of ½-inch plywood for the legs and one for the fascia, using clear plywood, free of knots or imperfections. Make the leg sections wide enough to extend from the edge of the marble surround far enough beyond the edge of the brick facing to overlap the flanking studs. Make the fascia section wide enough to span the legs and high enough to cover the top edge of the brick facing. Glue the sections together, aligning the long side of the fascia with the top of the legs, and fasten them on the back with corrugated fasteners spaced 3 inches apart.

To calculate the width of the returns, measure the distance between the wall and the fireplace surface that protrudes farthest from the wall—in this case, the surface of the marble surround. Add ¾ inch, to allow for the ½-inch thickness of the plywood frame plus ¼ inch for adjustment. Then, using this measurement, cut two returns, the same height as the legs. Glue and nail the returns to the back edge of the frame, using fourpenny (1½-inch) finishing nails *(inset)*.

2 **Attaching the trim.** Beginning 2¾ inches down from the top of the frame, wrap a strip of 3½-inch-wide baseboard molding around the front and two sides of the frame, mitering the corners. Glue and nail the molding to the frame, using ½-inch wire brads. Directly below the baseboard molding, wrap 2¼-inch-wide oval molding around the frame, mitering the corners and securing it to the frame in the same way.

Attach a strip of 3-inch-wide shingle molding below the oval molding, but instead of wrapping it around the frame, bring it down along the outer edge of each leg; miter it at the corners *(inset)*. Sand the joints lightly to smooth them.

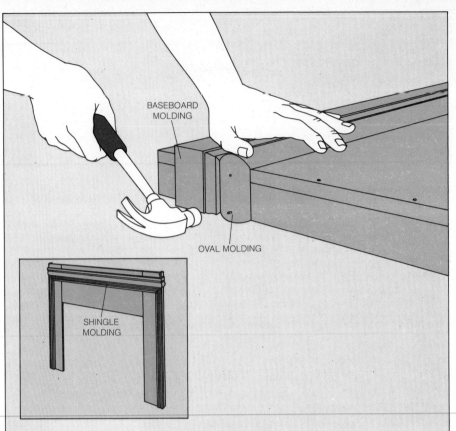

BASEBOARD MOLDING

OVAL MOLDING

SHINGLE MOLDING

3 **Completing the shelf.** Glue and nail 2¾-inch dentil molding to the baseboard molding. Then construct a shelf rimmed with half-round molding; the shelf should overhang the outer face of the dentil molding 4¼ inches on the front and sides. Join the shelf to the top of the frame with glue and fourpenny (1½-inch) finishing nails 8 inches apart; set the shelf flush with the back of the frame, centered between the sides.

Cut 4⅝ inch crown molding to fit around the frame under the shelf, following the mitering instructions in Step 2, page 112. Glue and nail it to the dentil, and toenail it to the underside of the shelf *(inset)*. The shelf should protrude beyond the edge of the crown molding 1½ inches. Sand the joints lightly to smooth them.

DENTIL

CROWN MOLDING   SHELF

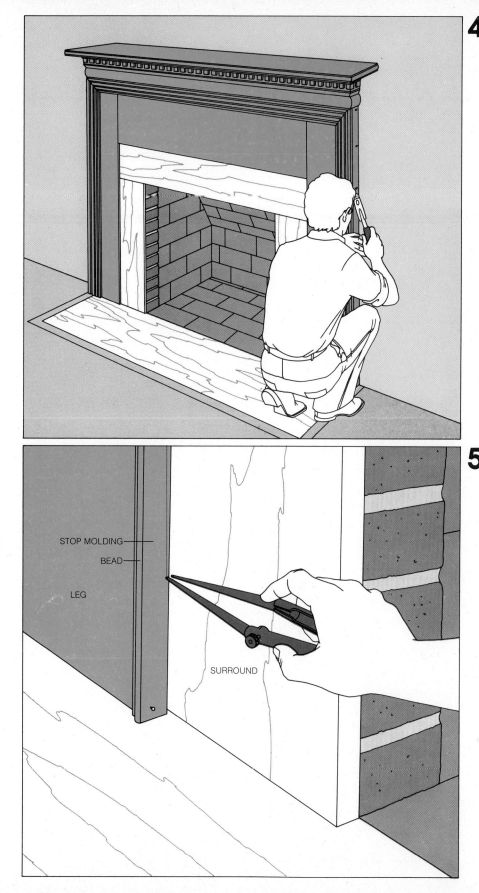

STOP MOLDING

BEAD

LEG

SURROUND

4 **Attaching the mantel to the wall.** Fasten a 2-by-2 cleat to the brick facing and, with a helper, lift the mantel into position against the fireplace. To seat the returns flush against the wall, cut the edges of the returns to fit snugly against the contours of the wall, using a rasp, a file or sandpaper. Nail the top of the shelf to the cleat with sixpenny (2-inch) finishing nails spaced 8 inches apart; then toenail the returns to the studs that flank the facing. Countersink the nails and fill the holes with wood putty.

To cover the gap between the marble surround and the plywood frame, cut three strips of stop molding to fit the inside edges of the two legs and the fascia; use beaded stop molding ⅜ inch thick and wide enough to cover the space between the face of the surround and the face of the frame. Miter the corners of the molding.

5 **Finishing the mantel.** Install one strip of stop molding temporarily with two small wire brads at the inside edge of one leg of the frame. Butt the back of the molding against the highest point of the surround, and line up the beaded front edge parallel with the face of the frame. Set the legs of a scribing compass to the width of the widest gap between the surround and the back of the molding. Then, starting at the top of the molding—with one leg of the compass on the molding and the other on the surface of the surround—scribe a line down the length of the molding, marking the corresponding contours of the surround.

Remove the molding and use a jig saw to contour the back edge of the molding, finishing the job with a shaped wood file, if necessary. Then glue and nail the molding to the edge of the frame with ½-inch wire brads. Repeat for the two other strips of molding, along the top and the opposite leg. Countersink the nails and fill the holes with wood putty; sand the joints lightly to smooth them. Finish the mantel as desired.

The Care and Feeding of a Fire

Back to basics. Although powered wood-splitting machines make short work of converting logs into firewood, using a sledge hammer and a steel wedge provides more exercise. Accomplished either way, log splitting speeds the wood's drying time and exposes its resinous core, thus causing it to ignite more quickly and burn better.

Heating with wood is likely to involve a series of anachronistic chores that seem more properly associated with Grandfather's day—felling trees, splitting logs, stacking a woodpile, setting a fire and keeping it going 24 hours a day, acting as a chimney sweep. Some of these tasks summon up images of backbreaking labor. But as the following pages show, many formerly arduous tasks associated with wood fires can now be accomplished with ease and dispatch.

The chain saw has made the two-man bucksaw obsolete as a way of turning trees into logs. With a rented power splitter the logs can be reduced to firewood three to four times faster than with a wedge and a sledge. The most revolutionary change in job description is in the cleaning of a chimney. What was once done from the rooftop by small boys—often naked to keep their clothes from snagging in the narrow flues—can now be done from the living room with long-handled brushes in relatively soot-free comfort, using the method described on page 120.

In one respect, however, the work associated with wood heat may have been simpler in Grandfather's day: Grandfather probably had a wood lot that supplied him with all the wood he needed. But even this advantage has a modern counterpart. With the growing interest in wood heat, government agencies will help interested customers acquire wood from public lands. The U.S. Forest Service, which is responsible for 154 national forests, will issue a permit to collect dead or downed trees from their lands, and many state forests will do the same. The cost usually is nominal—a few dollars per cord—and sometimes the wood is free.

If you have a few extra acres, forest services and agricultural extension services will even help you develop and manage your own wood lot, either from scratch (sometimes they will sell you seedlings) or by selectively thinning and encouraging trees that are already there. A ranger will often walk your land with you, advising you which species of trees to plant for the best yield, not only in terms of cords but also of heat output. (The chart on page 125 shows that hickory, for example, has cord for cord about twice the heating potential of poplar or white pine.)

What these public servants will not do, of course, is help you harvest the crop. An experienced woodsman can cut, buck, split and stack as much as four cords of wood a day; no amateur, not even one in good physical condition, can hope to match that production rate. But with practice you can probably reach a cord per day—and at that rate, even if you live in Canada or the northern United States you can lay in an average winter's wood supply, 7 to 10 cords, in four or five brisk autumn weekends.

The Mechanics of Maintaining a Perfect Fire

From first blaze to glowing embers, a wood fire can be a warm and romantic way to take the chill off an autumn evening, or it can be an auxiliary source of heat on a cold and blustery winter day. To build such a fire, all you need is some good dry wood, a match and a basic understanding of what makes a fire catch and keep going.

The best wood for a fire is a well-seasoned, dense wood, such as oak, hickory or locust. Freshly cut wood, roughly half water, will smolder when lighted, producing a good deal of smoke and little flame. Even worse, it will cause a rapid build-up of creosote in the flue.

For proper combustion, a continuous flow of air across and between the logs is needed. To start this air flow, warm the air in the flue by holding a torch of rolled-up newspaper directly beneath the opened damper. The warmed air will rise, pulling fresh air into the firebox. If the fire has been well laid, a single match will then ignite the paper and kindling, and thereafter, the heat of the fire will be enough to keep it self-sustaining.

To carry the fire through its various stages of combustion (opposite), you will need wood of various sizes—kindling and quarter-logs during the initial stages,

half-logs and full logs as the fire increases in intensity. Keeping three logs on the fire makes it easy to sustain. The logs should be placed close together but with narrow air spaces between them; they will then reflect heat onto each other, and the spaces will encourage the circulation of the air the logs need to burn.

Although an open fire in a fireplace is never a particularly efficient form of heat, care in tending it can improve its performance. Moving the fire forward in the firebox allows more heat to radiate into the room. Ashes banked against the back wall perform a similar function; they absorb heat and reflect it back into the room. A bed of ashes under the grate will also reflect heat against the logs, making them burn hotter. Be sure that the bed is not too high: It will cut off the fire's air supply. At night these ashes can be used to cover the glowing coals, preserving them to start the next day's fire.

Setting and tending a fire in a wood stove vary with the design of the stove, though the principles are the same as those for a fireplace. The best-laid fire is one that fills the entire firebox with burning wood, which means arranging the kindling and firewood to suit the stove's shape (opposite). Thereafter, tending the

fire is largely a matter of regulating the draft so that the volatile gases leaving the wood are completely burned. This is done by manipulation of the vents and the dampers.

Stoves differ in their venting arrangements, however, depending on whether they operate on updrafts or downdrafts. On a standard updraft stove, the vents are typically on the front—one at the fire level, one just above or below that level. On a downdraft stove, the vents are always on the top, above the fire.

During the initial firing, the vents and damper are opened wide to accelerate the draft. On an airtight stove, at this stage, the door is generally left ajar. Then, when there is a strong fire and a good bed of coals, the vents and damper are closed most of the way, to slow the fire and extend its heat; you will have to experiment with your stove to find the exact settings for the heat you need.

At night, if you add a large log and leave the vents barely open, the fire will continue to burn slowly until morning. It should then be fired up to intense heat: Open the vents wide and put in more wood, in order to burn off the creosote deposits that will have accumulated in the flue during the night.

Tools for tending an open fire. This fireplace is equipped with the basic accessories needed to keep the fire safely contained and make it easy to manage. A wide grate supports the wood and allows air to circulate around and beneath the fire. A fire screen keeps any popping coals safely inside the firebox. A set of fire tools should include a poker at least 28 inches long for stirring up the fire and opening new drafts among the embers, tongs to move and turn the logs, a shovel to pick up ashes or hot coals, and a brush for sweeping up ashes. Fireproof gloves are essential for protecting your hands while you tend a roaring fire. Bellows are useful to fan dying embers or to increase the air flow as a fire is kindled, and a wood basket is handy for keeping extra wood ready for feeding the fire.

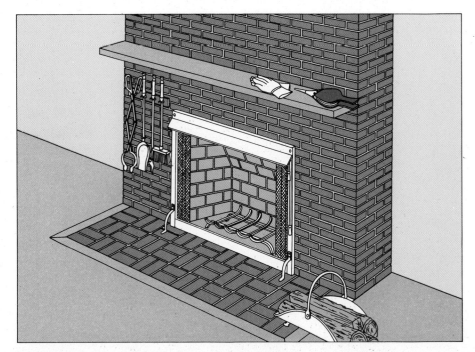

Setting and Tending a Fire by the Hearth

Creating a lasting fire. One match will start a fire when newspaper, logs and kindling are carefully arranged *(below, left)*. Several pages of newspaper, torn into inch-wide shreds, are spread under the grate. Two logs rest on top of the grate, 3 inches apart; kindling loosely fills the space between them—small pieces at the bottom, larger splits at the top. A third log rests above the other two, separated from them by two crosswise splits, to allow air to circulate.

After the kindling has ignited the logs, the fire will need only occasional attention. It should always contain at least three logs *(below, center)*, and they should be placed close enough together that the flames are burning no higher than 1 inch above the log that is on top. Banking the ashes against the back wall and underneath the grate, in order to cradle the coals that drop through, will help to keep the fire going for the longest possible time.

To keep the coals alive through the night, the burning logs are set in an upright position against the sides and toward the back of the firebox *(below, right)*, using fire tongs and a pair of heat-proof gloves. Then the hot embers underneath the grate are buried in a bed of ashes, and the damper is closed as far as possible while still permitting smoke to escape up the chimney. Remember to close the fire screen, which has been omitted here for the sake of clarity.

Techniques of Firing Up Four Types of Stove

Shaping the fire to the stove. Regardless of the type of stove, a fire in a wood stove starts with shredded newspaper, kindling and small splits of wood. But different stove shapes call for different arrangements of kindling and splits to make a fire that fills the firebox. In a tall stove, such as a potbelly *(far left, top)*, a layer of newspaper is covered with a layer of dry twigs and sticks; small splits are then arranged tepee fashion above the newspaper and kindling. In a long narrow stove *(near left, top)*, the kindling is laid atop a bed of newspaper running the length of the stove, then covered with a latticework of splits, laid diagonally to carry the fire from front to back. In a square stove *(far left, bottom)*, the splits are arranged log-cabin fashion over the bed of newspaper and kindling.

In a downdraft stove *(near left, bottom)*, because the fire will burn from top to bottom, the components are arranged in reverse order. Logs are placed at the bottom, with a cross layer of smaller splits atop them, followed by a layer of kindling covered with shredded newspaper.

Engineering a Clean Sweep of the Chimney Flue

If it were possible to burn wood completely, a flue would never need cleaning; the only materials that would go up the chimney would be water and carbon dioxide. But complete combustion is never achieved and, paradoxically, the more efficiently a fireplace or stove burns, the more likely it is to send unburned residues up the flue. These residues leave the firebox as soot—unburned carbon particles—and as a chemical vapor, some of which condenses into sticky creosote on the surface of the flue much as water vapor forms dew on a glass of iced tea in summer.

Flues caked with soot and creosote—both flammable—are major causes of chimney fires, which unfortunately are not always contained within the chimney. Flaming debris can set fire to the roof or crack the flue liner, allowing the flame to escape and ignite the frame of the house. You can prevent chimney fires by sweeping the chimney, and the procedures shown on the following pages keep the house clean—the trickiest part of the job. In this professional method, fireplace chimneys are swept safely from below. Vertical metal flues, however, can be cleaned only from above.

Unfortunately, the only way to discover when a flue needs cleaning is to inspect it—inevitably a dirty job. Though the average chimney needs sweeping only once every two years, it should be inspected more often. The flue of a fireplace that gets heavy and continuous use, or of a stove that is airtight, may need to be cleaned monthly. Monthly inspections are in fact a good idea, at least until you become familiar with the rate at which your particular stove or fireplace collects deposits. When the build-up is more than ⅛ inch thick, the flue needs cleaning, and so does the smoke chamber of a fireplace.

The cleaning itself is fairly straightforward. In a masonry fireplace chimney being cleaned from below, you must first remove the damper plate from the fireplace throat and then, to keep soot out of the house, cover the fireplace opening with plastic sheeting. A small opening in the plastic allows you to work. For a stove with a metal flue, which is cleaned from above, you must partially dismantle the bottom of the flue pipe and tape a catch bag over it to collect debris. The same is true of a freestanding fireplace, unless you can reach up to remove its damper plate and clean it from below—as you would a masonry fireplace.

The special brushes needed for sweeping flues are made of wire and are shaped to fit snugly into common-sized flues. If your house is of recent construction, it most likely has an 8-by-12-inch or 12-by-12-inch flue. Older houses may have odd sizes, so when in doubt, measure the flue. This can usually be done by reaching up from below, using a retractable ruler or a length of wire to measure the span of the opening. You can also measure the flue from the roof—if you find more than one flue emerging from the chimney, be sure to measure the one connected to the stove or fireplace. Remember when measuring a masonry flue that the actual inside dimensions are smaller than the nominal dimensions.

A flue brush operated from above can either be lowered on a rope or be pushed down on sections of flexible rod made of fiberglass, plastic or cane. From below, the brush can be used only with the rods, which are in sections 3 to 6 feet long and are joined with screw or snap couplings.

If you are working from above, using a rope, you will have to buy a loop adapter for the brush, plus lead sash weights to add to the brush. In addition to the flue brush, you will also need a long-handled pot brush. The pot brush is used for cleaning fireplace smoke chambers and the inside of stoves. If the flue is coated with shiny, baked-on creosote, you will also need a steel scraper.

Although chimney-sweeping equipment is becoming more widely available as wood heating becomes more common, you may have trouble finding some items. What you do find may be flimsy—some chimney-sweeping kits, for example, have fiberglass rods too thin for the job. Similarly, flue cleaners that employ a flexible flat plastic scraper matched to the flue size are regarded with skepticism by experienced professionals. If proper tools are unavailable locally, you can order them directly from firms such as the Worcester Brush Company in Worcester, Massachusetts, or from Mazzeo's Chimney Sweep Suppliers in Rockland, Maine, which imports British chimney-sweeping equipment and specializes in the steel scrapers that remove hardened creosote.

Sweeping a Masonry Chimney from Below

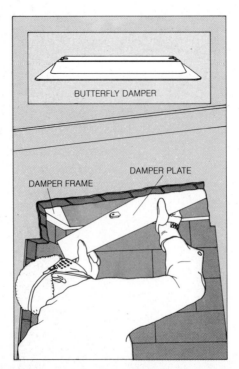

BUTTERFLY DAMPER

DAMPER PLATE

DAMPER FRAME

1 **Gaining access to the flue.** First remove the damper plate and the operating lever by detaching the lever from the plate and tilting the plate out of the frame. Most frequently a cotter pin holds the lever to the plate, and the plate simply rests on the frame. On a butterfly damper *(inset)*, metal straps may hold the plate's hinge pins against the frame. If so, in order to tilt the plate from its frame, you must remove one or both of the bolts that hold the straps. With the plate removed, look inside the smoke chamber—wearing goggles or using a mirror—to ascertain its size and shape and to locate the outlet for the flue.

If the damper plate is installed in such a way that it cannot be removed, swing it open as far as possible and see if there is enough room to push the sweeping brush through. If not, you will have to clean the chimney from the top.

2 **Sealing the fireplace opening.** Cut a sheet of 4-mil polyethelene sheeting slightly larger than the fireplace opening, and fasten it to the top of the opening with two tabs of duct tape. Then seal the entire edge of the plastic to the fireplace—top, bottom and sides—with continuous strips of duct tape. Cut an inverted T shape 15 inches wide and 10 inches high in the center of the plastic *(inset)*. Watch the flaps created by the cut; they should pull into the fireplace, indicating the presence of an updraft that will carry loosened soot up and out the flue.

If there is no updraft, create one by closing off the room, then opening one window and pulling in air with a fan. Protect the area before the hearth with a layer of newspapers or an old sheet.

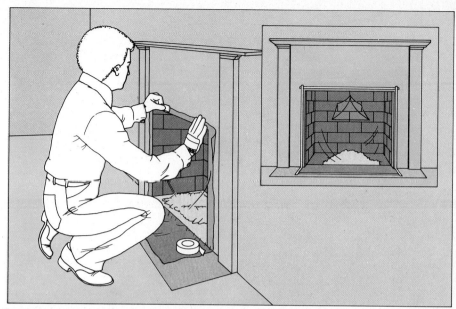

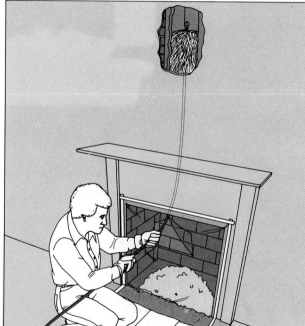

3 **Sweeping the flue.** Attach the flue brush to a section of rod; push the brush through the opening in the plastic, past the damper and up into the flue. Work the brush up and down until the noise of falling debris subsides. Then move the brush up to clean the next section of flue, attaching rods as needed until the brush reaches to the top of the flue. Finally, pull the brush back down to the smoke chamber, detaching all but the first section of the rod.

4 **Cleaning the smoke chamber.** With a flue brush, scrub the walls of the smoke chamber vigorously to loosen deposits; then finish the job by going over the walls a second time with a pot brush. To remove the debris, slip a large double-thick paper bag through the opening in the plastic, into the fireplace. Hold the bag open with one hand while you use the other hand to sweep accumulated soot and creosote from the smoke shelf into the bag. Then use a dust pan to shovel debris from the fireplace floor into the bag. If you do not intend to scrape glazed creosote from the flue, remove the plastic cover from the fireplace. Pull off the duct tape slowly if the frame of the fireplace is painted, to avoid damaging the paint. Roll up and discard the protective newspaper or sheeting.

Removing a Coating of Glazed Creosote

Using a scraper. After loose soot and creosote have been removed with a brush, you may still need to remove crusts of creosote. Attach a steel scraper to a rod section, and slip it through the plastic sheet, up into the flue. Add rod sections to extend the scraper to the top of the flue, and then work your way down, scraping up and down the flue walls in repeated 3-foot-long strokes. Roll your wrists clockwise on the upstroke, causing the scraper to move about within the flue, then pull it straight down. Listen for falling debris; when the sound diminishes, work on the next 3-foot section of flue. If the chimney configuration permits, use a mirror to check your progress. Remove the material that has fallen onto the smoke shelf and fireplace floor. Then, a month later, check the smoke shelf again; after the flue has been scraped, hot gases may undercut some of the remaining creosote and cause it to fall onto the shelf.

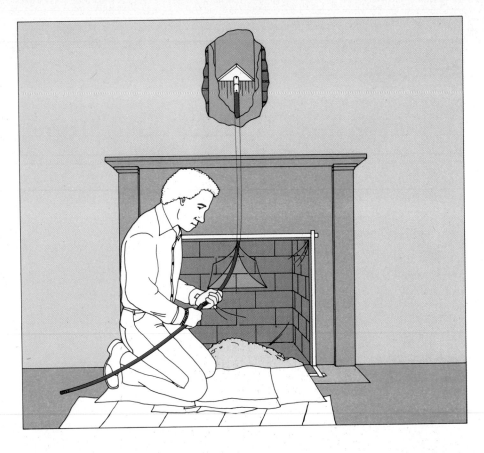

Sweeping a Vertical Metal Chimney Pipe

1 Opening the bottom of the flue. For a stove or freestanding fireplace with a round flue opening at the back, undo any screws holding the elbow section of stovepipe to the opening, then undo the screws holding the damper section of pipe to the section above it. Remove this loosened portion of pipe. With duct tape, fasten a large double-thick paper bag to the open end of the pipe, to catch debris.

For a stove or fireplace with a flue opening on the top, undo the screws that hold the stovetop to the opening and the screws that hold the pipe to the collar at the ceiling. Shift the pipe upward about 2½ inches and retighten the ceiling connection. Then remove the section of pipe containing the damper, and fasten a paper bag to the open end of the pipe.

Caution: When disassembling a stovepipe flue, determine beforehand that its weight is not supported solely by its connection to the heating unit. The section that passes through the ceiling should be supported there as well.

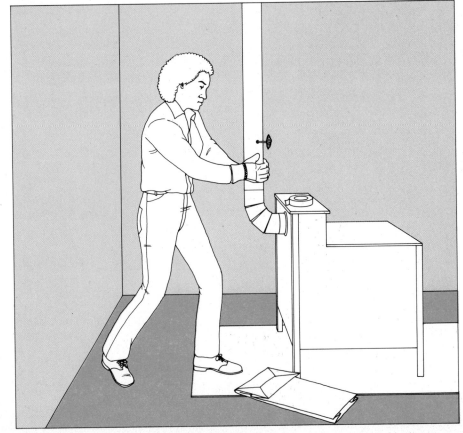

2 **Sweeping the flue.** On the roof, remove the chimney cap if there is one; if the stovepipe extends too high above the roof for you to work the sweeping brush up and down, remove a section or more of the pipe. Lower a weighted brush, or brush fitted with rods, to the bottom of the flue. Have a helper stationed at the bottom of the flue to warn you when the brush gets close to the catch bag. Work your way up the flue slowly, using up-and-down strokes. When you have finished sweeping the main portion of the flue, clean the dismantled portions on the ground. Then carefully remove the catch bag and reassemble the flue. Finally, clean the interior of the firebox with a pot brush.

ADAPTER

SASH WEIGHT

Cleaning a Horizontal Pipe

Fabricating a special catch-bag assembly. To clean a section of flue that runs horizontally to meet a vertical stovepipe extending upward outside a house, you need two catch bags—one to collect the bulk of the debris, the other to prevent soot from sifting into the house. Attach the first bag to the bottom of the T section joining the two runs of pipe outside the house, removing the cap on the T section for this purpose; tape the bag to the opening *(inset)*.

Indoors, disconnect the horizontal pipe from the vertical pipe leading down to the stove or freestanding fireplace. Insert the flue brush and one section of rod in the open end of the horizontal pipe. Prepare a second catch bag by cutting a 2-inch slit in the side of a heavy plastic garbage bag; reinforce the slit with duct tape, and slide it over the rod. Tape the bag top to the open end of the pipe and, working slowly, push the brush back and forth, gradually forcing the debris through the pipe into the outside catch bag.

When the pipe is clean, draw the brush slowly back, to avoid pumping soot through the slit in the inside catch bag. Ease the brush into the bag, and remove the bag from the pipe. Clean the remaining parts, then reassemble the flue.

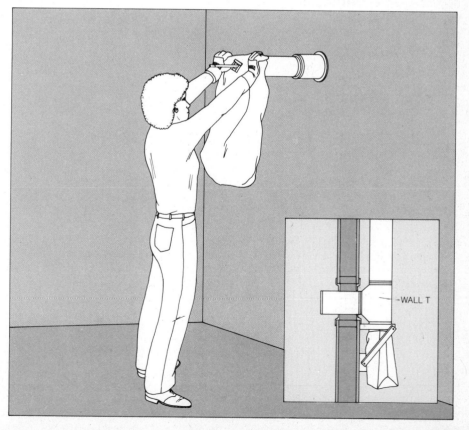

WALL T

A Guide to Buying and Storing Firewood

Buying wood fuel for a fireplace or a wood stove takes more than money. The purchaser should know exactly what kind of wood is needed, where to get it, and how to evaluate its quality.

The simplest way to buy wood is from a dealer, generally listed in the classified telephone directory under "Firewood." Dealers sell wood by the cord. A full cord is a stack that is 8 feet long, 4 feet high and 4 feet deep—in other words, 128 cubic feet of stacked firewood. Usually the logs are cut 2 feet long, but for slightly more money you can have them sawed into shorter lengths to fit your fireplace or stove. A partial cord, called a face cord or a rick, is the same length and height as a regular cord, but it can be anywhere from 1 to 3 feet deep.

When you buy a cord or a rick of wood from a dealer, you can either haul it home yourself—if you have a pickup truck and a strong back—or, for an additional charge, have it delivered.

You may have a choice between unseasoned and seasoned wood. Unseasoned wood will cost less, but the logs will be 4 feet long, unsplit and green—that is, freshly cut. Green wood has a high moisture content—about 60 per cent—so it usually must be seasoned by drying for 6 to 12 months, or until it reaches a moisture content of about 20 per cent, before it is ready to be burned. If you burn green logs, the heat of the fire will turn the water in the wood into steam, and in most cases the steam will condense in the flue, leaving deposits that will eventually turn into creosote, which is flammable.

To season green wood, you should split it by one of the methods on pages 132-133 so that it will dry faster, then stack it as shown below. Stacking it in a crisscross pattern further speeds drying.

Seasoned logs will be split and ready to use when you buy them. The logs will look dark and withered, and their ends will have cracks that radiate from the center. To test wood for dryness, toss two logs into the air so that they collide. Dry logs make a sharp, ringing sound; you will hear a dull thud if the wood is green.

Before buying wood, you must also decide on the type you want. Hardwoods, which generally come from deciduous, broad-leaved trees, are dense and burn evenly for a long time, although they may be slow to catch fire. Softwoods, which generally come from evergreen trees, are less dense, burn faster, and produce less heat per cord than hardwoods. The softwoods, because they contain resins, are also more prone to leave a creosote deposit in a chimney flue; if you burn softwood, check and clean your chimney frequently (page 120).

Dealers commonly sell cords composed of 80 per cent hardwood and 20 per cent softwood. You can order a full cord of a single type of wood, if you like, although you may have to pay a premium for it.

When the wood reaches your yard, it should be stacked in a sunny spot, well away from the house, and supported off the ground as shown below. This arrangement allows air to circulate around the wood; it also discourages termites and other wood-eating insects from crawling into the woodpile, or worse, into your house. If you buy unseasoned logs, a solar dryer built around the woodpile (opposite, top) can shorten the drying time to about three months.

Although firewood dealers are the handiest source of wood fuel, they are not the only source. Every autumn, vendors—usually from nearby farms—drive trucks through suburban neighborhoods, peddling loads of logs. Before you buy, learn to identify the common local types of wood. Be sure you know the current price for a cord of wood, and check the logs for dryness. If possible, measure the length, height and depth of the stack in the truck, and compare these measurements with the volume of a cord.

Other sources for firewood, if you are willing to do your own collecting and cutting, are found on public lands. In many state and national forests, dead or diseased trees are marked for removal and can be carted away free or for a nominal charge. Sawmills, city dumps, and sites cleared for utility lines or roads are also sources of free firewood.

Wood, of course, is not the only material that can be burned in a fireplace or a wood stove. Logs made of compressed wood chips are convenient but expensive. You can also burn rolled-up newspapers, although the paper produces a lot of smoke. The newspapers should be soaked in soapy water overnight—the fat in the soap helps the paper ignite—and then rolled tightly, with a device sold at most hardware stores, and dried.

Stacking and Seasoning Firewood in the Yard

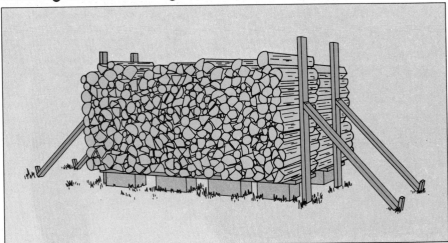

A sturdy support for a cord of wood. A simple frame for a cord—a stack 8 feet long, 4 feet high and 4 feet deep—begins with two rows of concrete blocks, spaced 2 feet apart; the four blocks in each row are 1 foot apart, end to end. An 8-foot 2-by-10 rests on each row; logs are stacked on the boards. Two vertical 2-by-4s, driven 1 foot into the ground, are braced by diagonal 2-by-4s. The braces are beveled and nailed at the upper end to the vertical supports and butted against 2-by-2 stakes at the lower end. The stack can be covered with a sheet of plastic.

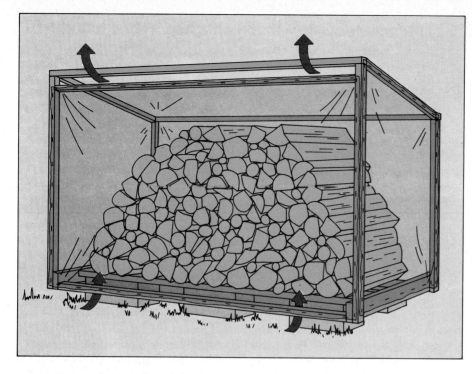

A solar dryer for speedy seasoning. A solar dryer with a wood frame and clear plastic-film walls traps heat from the sun to season green wood in about three months. The base is made of two rows of concrete blocks, with three blocks spaced about 1 foot apart in each row. A 6-foot-long 2-by-10 rests atop each row of blocks, and 3-foot-long 2-by-4s are nailed across the ends of the 2-by-10s. The green wood is then stacked loosely on this base.

To support the plastic walls, vertical 2-by-2s are nailed to 2-by-4s at the four bottom corners of the dryer; the 2-by-2s at the front are 4 feet high, and those at the back are 3 feet high. Horizontals cut from 2-by-2 lumber connect all four corners at the top of the dryer, as well as the corners forming the front and back of the base, and provide stapling surfaces for the 4-mil polyethylene film that covers the walls and roof of the dryer. Below the top front, a second horizontal 2-by-2 creates a 2-inch opening that allows air to escape. Detach the plastic to remove the wood.

Getting the Most Heat for Your Money

Heat value per cord	Type of wood	Splitting and burning characteristics
High: 24-30 million BTUs	Hickory (hardwood)	Moderately hard to split; moderately hard to ignite; makes long-lasting coals
	Beech (hardwood)	Hard to split; hard to ignite; burns unseasoned
	Sugar maple (hardwood)	Moderately hard to split; hard to ignite; fragrant
	Oak (hardwood)	Moderately hard to split; hard to ignite; makes long-lasting coals
	Ash (hardwood)	Moderately easy to split; moderately hard to ignite; burns unseasoned
Medium: 16-23 million BTUs	Elm (hardwood)	Very hard to split; moderately hard to ignite; smokes moderately
	Gum (hardwood)	Hard to split; moderately hard to ignite; smokes moderately
	Sycamore (hardwood)	Hard to split; moderately hard to ignite; smokes moderately
	Red maple (hardwood)	Easy to split; moderately hard to ignite; makes long-lasting coals
	Douglas fir (softwood)	Easy to split; easy to ignite; smokes heavily; sparks heavily
	Piñon (softwood)	Easy to split; easy to ignite; smokes heavily
Low: 13-15 million BTUs	Poplar (hardwood)	Easy to split; moderately hard to ignite; burns quickly; sparks heavily
	Spruce (softwood)	Easy to split; easy to ignite; sparks heavily
	Aspen (hardwood)	Easy to split; easy to ignite; smokes moderately; sparks heavily
	White pine (softwood)	Easy to split; easy to ignite; smokes moderately

The qualities of common firewoods. The hardwoods and softwoods above are listed in descending order according to their heat value, measured in BTUs (British thermal units). Other characteristics of each wood are listed at the right. Not listed are fruit woods such as apple and pear, which are scarce but are desirable because of their high heat value and pleasant aroma. Certain hardwoods such as ash, beech and hickory contain less moisture and can be burned even when green—unseasoned—without creating an unusual creosote build-up.

Harvesting Trees Safely and Expeditiously

Anyone who uses wood as a source of heat will tell you there is plenty of heat to be found in converting a tree into burning logs—body heat as well as wood heat. Indeed, the task of felling trees with a two-man crosscut saw is enjoying a comeback as a popular form of exercise.

Most people settle for a gasoline-and-oil-powered chain saw, with which a tree can be felled in minutes. The saw also simplifies two follow-up jobs—limbing and bucking. Limbing is the process of trimming off limbs; bucking is cutting the trunk into logs of suitable length for a fireplace or a stove.

Logs more than 10 or 12 inches in diameter must then be split for efficient burning. This can be done by hand with a splitting maul, with a 6- to 10-pound sledge hammer and a pair of steel splitting wedges, or with a sledge hammer and a cone-shaped wedge that can split a log into several pieces with a single blow. The splitting maul has a wedgelike head that is swung down into the log, splitting it into pieces more easily than a conventional ax can do.

If you have a great many logs to split, you may prefer to rent a mechanical splitter. There are two common versions.

One splits logs on a spinning cone; the other uses hydraulic power to ram the log against a stationary wedge (page 133).

Though the choice of tools is optional, there are certain time-honored practices in the felling of a tree. The diameter of the tree dictates the manner in which the cuts are made. If the diameter is less than the length of the chain saw's guide bar the tree can be felled in three simple cuts (page 127). If the diameter is greater than the length of the bar, a more complex cut is needed (page 128). But if the diameter is more than twice the length of the chain saw's guide bar, the job of felling

Choosing and Using a Chain Saw

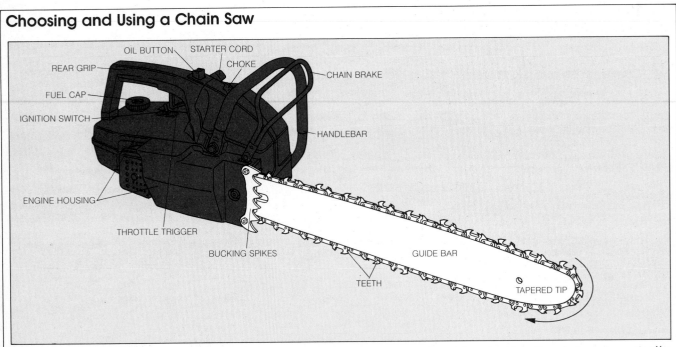

The cutting action of a chain saw is carried out by small teeth on a linked chain, like a bicycle chain, spinning around a 9- to 16-inch steel guide bar. The operator controls the saw from two grips on the engine housing—a handlebar at the front, which positions the saw, and a rear grip, which helps push the saw into the wood. The chain's speed is controlled by the throttle trigger; all cuts are made at full throttle.

A chain saw can be a very dangerous tool because its cutting chain spins so rapidly and is completely exposed. Most accidents result from a kickback during a cut. The tip of the guide bar makes unexpected contact with other wood or with the ground, causing the guide bar to jump back toward the operator. A taper on the tip of some chain-saw guide bars reduces the area of revolving chain that might contact another object during the cut and kick back.

But these tapered guide-bar tips do not prevent kickback entirely. Consequently, many chain saws are designed with a chain brake that also helps prevent injuries. Should the guide bar kick back, the chain brake will hit the wrist of the hand grasping the handle-

bar, braking the chain automatically.

Chain saws powered by gasoline and oil are started with an ignition switch and a starter cord. A choke is used to start a cold engine. Pumping the oil button lubricates the chain and guide bar. Electric chain saws are used mostly for lighter sawing at home.

If you operate a chain saw, take these precautions. Always wear a hard hat, safety goggles and leather work gloves when felling and limbing trees or bucking logs. Since a chain saw is extremely noisy, use ear protectors if you will be working with it for some time.

the tree should be left to a professional.

Before a cut is made, assess its aftermath. It is easiest to fell a tree toward its natural lean, but this is not always best. Another tree may be in the way, or the natural line of fall may cross a power line. Sometimes it is possible, with wedges and a special tapered cut, to fell the tree 90° away from its natural lean, provided it is not leaning too severely. If the lean is severe, you can use a block and tackle to guide the tree as it falls. If the tree has no discernible lean, it will fall in the direction of the notch cut.

Safety is always the primary concern. Avoid felling trees on steep slopes; the follow-up jobs of limbing and bucking are difficult and dangerous in such loca-

tions. Also, before you fell a tree, clear the area of other people and make sure that you have an escape route, away from any possible line of fall.

It is common practice, after the tree is felled, to remove all the limbs except those underneath. They will hold the tree trunk off the ground for easier sawing; they can be trimmed off later. Begin limbing at the treetop and work down, taking off the biggest limbs last. Then saw the larger limbs and trunk into logs.

It is important to prevent two sections of log from pinching together and binding the guide bar. Note the stresses that will be put on the cut by its location, and select the appropriate cutting technique. Also, if you are cutting a small tree into

logs on flat ground, it is usually easier to make a series of cuts, called overbucks, on the top, all along its length. Then roll the tree over and complete the cuts from the other side. Or, to keep the moving chain off the ground, prop up the trunk with a good-sized log.

The final step, splitting the logs, can also be made easier with a few tricks. Split logs from bottom to top; to identify the bottom, check the direction of the stubs of limbs—they will point to the top. Take advantage of an existing crack or check, radiating from the center, by starting a wedge there; if the grain bends, split along the line of the bend rather than against it. Finally, you can split logs with greatest ease when they are frozen.

Felling a Tree of Small Diameter

1 Cutting a notch. Make two cuts to form a notch on the face of the tree—the side toward which it leans and therefore will fall. To make the first cut, hold the guide bar horizontal, about 1½ feet above the ground, with the engine housing resting against the tree. Bring the engine to full throttle and drive the guide bar into the tree, swinging it in a horizontal arc. Cut one third of the way through the trunk (*near right*). Reduce the engine speed to half throttle and remove the guide bar from the cut.

Hold the guide bar at a 45° downward angle to the first cut, positioning the saw so that the second cut will meet the end of the first. Make the cut by pushing the guide bar evenly along its diagonal path (*far right*), not in an arc as you did before. Remove the guide bar from the cut, and knock out the wedge-shaped piece of wood.

2 Making the felling cut. With a helper stationed nearby to tap you with a stick in case of danger from above, make a horizontal cut on the side of the tree directly opposite the notch, about 2 inches above the bottom face of the notch. The cut should end approximately 2 inches short of the back of the notch, creating a diagonal hinge. Then the trunk will pivot on the hinge, causing the tree to fall. The instant the tree begins to move—your helper will tap you—release the throttle, withdraw the guide bar, switch off the engine and move to safety.

FACE

DIRECTION OF FALL

NOTCH CUT

HINGE

DIRECTION OF FALL

Special Cuts for Downing a Large Tree

1 **Cutting a wide notch.** Position the chain saw horizontally, as for the first half of a notch cut *(page 127, Step 1)*. Make the first cut by rotating the guide bar into the tree for a distance equal to one third of its diameter. Then make a diagonal cut to meet the horizontal cut. Moving across the tree and working from the other side, make a companion pair of cuts, lining them up with the first pair to create a large notch across the entire face of the tree. Knock out the wedge-shaped piece of wood.

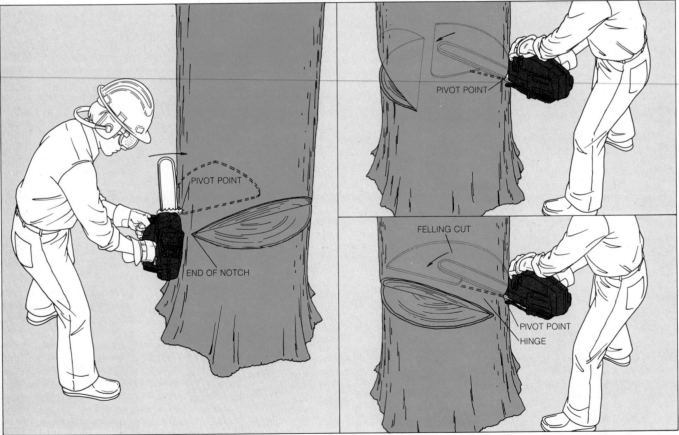

2 **Making a long hinge.** Rest the saw's engine housing against the tree about 2 inches behind one end of the notch; point the guide bar away from the notch, and hold it parallel to the ground on a line approximately 2 inches above the horizontal face of the notch. Then, using the engine housing as a pivot point, swing the guide bar in a horizontal arc through the tree trunk, end-

ing the cut when the guide bar is parallel to the back of the notch.

For the second cut, position the engine housing against the tree halfway around the trunk, with the guide bar pointing toward the first pivot point. Cut in an arc, ending the cut when the guide bar is almost perpendicular to the back of the

notch *(top right)*. Complete the hinge and final cut with the saw body at a third pivot point, directly opposite the first pivot point; the guide bar should be pointing toward the second pivot point. As before, cut in an arc. End the cut with the guide bar parallel to the back of the notch *(bottom right)*. As the tree begins to fall, remove the saw and move to safety as in Step 2, page 127.

Directing the Fall of a Small Tree

1 **Cutting an angled hinge.** To make a tree fall in a direction against its natural lean, cut a notch *(page 127, Step 1),* on the side of the tree facing the desired direction of fall. Then, opposite the notch, make a horizontal felling cut *(page 127, Step 2),* but cut at an angle so that one end is closer to the back of the notch than the other, creating a hinge with ends of unequal depth. The wider end of the hinge should be opposite the direction of the natural lean.

2 **Driving wedges to fell the tree.** Just next to the narrow end of the hinge, drive two wooden or plastic wedges into the felling cut; the wedges will shift the tree's center of gravity away from the natural direction of lean, forcing the tree to fall in the direction of the notch. If the tree does not fall, remove the wedge closest to the hinge by hitting it from the side with the sledge hammer. Deepen the felling cut slightly, then drive the wedge back into the cut.

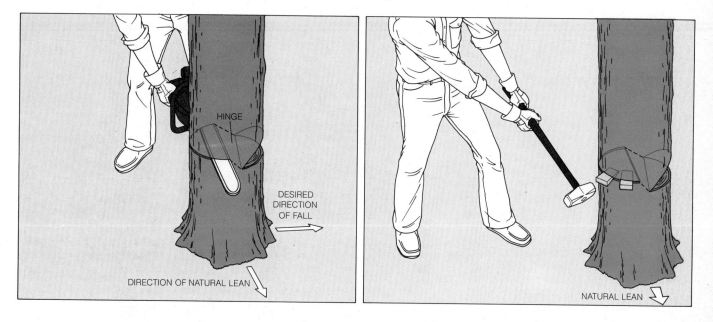

HINGE

DESIRED DIRECTION OF FALL

DIRECTION OF NATURAL LEAN

NATURAL LEAN

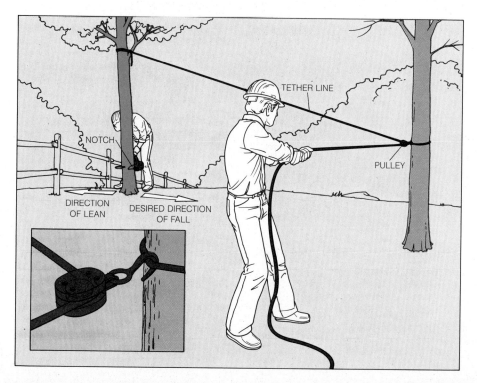

TETHER LINE

NOTCH

PULLEY

DIRECTION OF LEAN

DESIRED DIRECTION OF FALL

Guiding a Falling Tree with Block and Tackle

Attaching a tether line and pulley. Tie one end of a 1-inch Manila-rope tether line around the tree to be felled; fasten the line with a square knot as high on the trunk as you can reach. Run the line to a tree situated roughly in line with the desired direction of fall, and fasten a pulley assembly *(inset)* to its trunk, about 2 feet from the ground. Pass the tether line through the pulley and have a helper pull the line taut at a 90° angle. Make sure your helper is standing well away from the line of fall, at a distance at least twice the height of the tree being felled.

Cut a notch in line with the desired direction of fall *(page 127, Step 1)* and, as you are making the horizontal felling cut on the opposite side of the trunk, have your helper pull on the tether line to control the direction of fall.

Removing Limbs from a Felled Tree

Limbing the trunk. Starting at the top of the tree and standing on the side of the trunk opposite the limb being cut, set the guide bar parallel to the trunk and cut toward the bottom of the tree through the base of the limb. Do not let the tip of the guide bar hit the ground. Progress along the trunk, cutting off all the limbs on one side, then on the other, and finally on the top— holding the guide bar horizontal for the latter cuts. Leave the limbs on the underside intact, to support the trunk during bucking.

If the tree lies across a slight incline, brace the trunk by leaving several limbs beneath and on the downhill side to keep it from rolling; stand on the uphill side to make the limbing cuts. Adjust your stance to keep your legs away from the guide bar when cutting limbs on the uphill side.

Sawing a Tree Trunk into Fire-Sized Logs

1 **Beginning a bucking cut.** Cut a length suitable for your fireplace or wood stove by resting the saw's engine housing against the trunk, with the guide bar beneath the tree, and pivoting the housing against the tree. Swing the guide bar up to saw through roughly one third of the thickness of the trunk.

For a tree thicker than the length of the guide bar, repeat this cut from the other side of the tree.

2 **Finishing the bucking cut.** Rest the engine housing against the tree, guide bar across the top of the trunk and in line with the first bucking cut. Using the housing as a pivot, push the guide bar down through the wood to meet the first cut. Repeat the top cut from the opposite side of the trunk if necessary.

Repeat the bucking cuts along the length of the tree, dividing the trunk into 1½- to 3-foot logs. When you have finished, roll each log onto one side and saw off any remaining limbs.

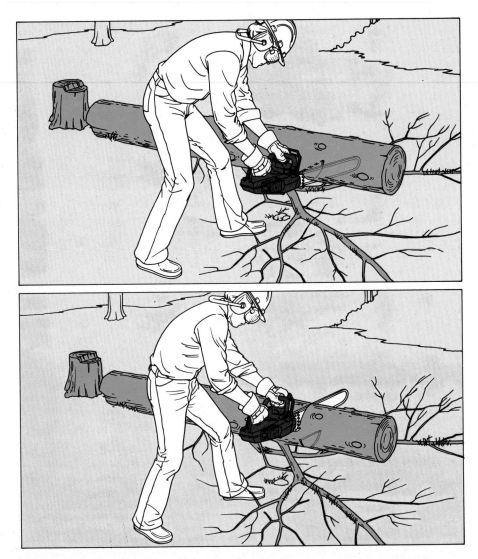

Cutting Logs in Special Situations

Bucking a tree that lies flat on the ground. Hold the guide bar horizontal over the top of the tree, and drive the guide bar straight down through half of the trunk. Stop the engine and, leaving the guide bar in the wood, tap a wooden wedge into the top of the cut to keep the log sections from binding the guide bar. Restart the engine and continue cutting downward, taking care to stop before the guide bar hits the ground. The log will probably break apart naturally; if it does not, give it a sharp kick to separate it.

For a slender tree that you can roll by hand, avoid the danger of hitting the ground with the guide bar by making top cuts halfway through the trunk all along the tree. Then roll the trunk over, and cut down again to meet each existing cut.

Bucking an unsupported section of trunk. When a section of trunk lacks a sufficient number of supporting points to remain horizontal after being cut, and it appears that the cut sections may fall toward the guide bar and pinch it, reverse the order of the bucking cuts. Make the first cut from the top through one third of the trunk. Then cut up from the underside.

Making angled bucking cuts. When a section of trunk is balanced in such a way that one cut section is likely to remain stationary while the other falls toward the guide bar, make the two bucking cuts at an angle, to prevent binding. Make the first cut from the top, angling it downward toward the section of the tree that will remain stationary, sawing one third of the way through the trunk. Then cut up from underneath at about the same angle.

FALLING SECTION

STATIONARY SECTION

Splitting Logs with a Sledge and a Wedge

Splitting a log with a sledge and a wedge. Set the log, bottom end up, on a splitting stump; hold a steel wedge against the top end of the log between the center and the edge, lining up the cutting edge of the wedge with the center of the log, and tap the wedge into the wood with a small sledge hammer until it will stand on its own *(below, left)*. If there is an open crack radiat- ing from the center of the log, use it as an en- tering point for the wedge. Then, with a full, overhead swing of a 6- to 12-pound long-handled sledge hammer, pound the wedge down into the log to split it *(below)*. For an especially large or hard-to-split log, repeat the procedure with a second wedge, working in a straight line across the center of the log until it splits.

Freeing a stuck wedge. To free a wedge that is jammed in the end of a log, tap a second wedge into the wood next to and in line with the stuck wedge. Then strike the second wedge with a small sledge, opening a crack wide enough to allow the first wedge to be released.

Whittling Down a Very Thick Log

Splitting away the perimeter of the log. For a log more than 18 inches in diameter, which may be difficult to split with one or two blows, first remove sections 4 to 6 inches thick around the perimeter of the log. For these peripheral splits, use a splitting maul or a wedge and a sledge hammer, with the edge of the tool entering the log perpendicular to its radius. Work around the log until the remaining core is narrow enough to split across the center *(inset)*.

Machines That Speed the Splitting Task

Using a cone-screw splitter. Hold the side of a 2- to 4-foot-long log diagonally against the point of the revolving cone, resting the log on the support bar *(below, left)*. As soon as the cone has seized the log, let go; the threaded point of the cone will draw the log toward the cone's wider base, causing the wood to split in half *(below, right)*. Remove the log halves and split them into quarter sections, if desired, by pushing the split face to each of the halves against the cone.

CONE

SUPPORT BAR

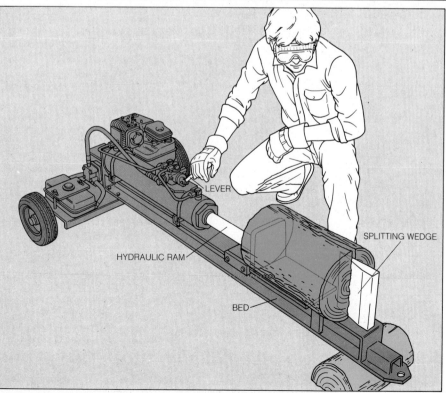

LEVER

HYDRAULIC RAM

BED

SPLITTING WEDGE

Using a hydraulic splitter. Level the bed of the splitter by propping the lower end on a solid base, such as a split log; then set a log up to 4 feet long on the bed, butting one end against the hydraulic ram. Steady the log with one hand, push down the lever, and let go of the log. The ram will drive the wood against the wedge.

To split a half log into quarters, lay the split face against the bed and activate the ram as before.

Picture Credits

The sources for the illustrations in this book are shown below. The drawings were created by Jack Arthur, Roger Essley, Charles Forsythe, John Jones, Dick Lee, John Martinez and Joan McGurren. Credits for the illustrations from left to right are separated by semicolons, from top to bottom by dashes.

Cover: Fil Hunter. 6: Fil Hunter. 9-11: Frederic F. Bigio from B-C Graphics. 13: Arezou Katoozian. 15-19: Frederic F. Bigio from B-C Graphics. 20-25: Walter Hilmers Jr. from HJ Commercial Art. 27-31: John Massey. 33: © Robert Perron, 1978, Moore Grover Harper, ar-chitects. 34, 35: © Robert Perron, 1980, Donnelley Erdman, architect; Aldo Ballo, Milan, Giotto Stoppino, architect—Emmett Bright, Rome, Charles Gianferrari, architect. 36, 37: Emmett Bright, Rome, Dmitri Coromilas, architect; © Robert Perron, 1977, Banwell White & Arnold, architects; © Mark Duran, 1981, Frank Lloyd Wright Foundation, architects—© Robert Perron, 1977, Banwell White & Arnold, architects. 38, 39: Norman McGrath, Moore Grover Harper, architects—Emmett Bright, Rome, Jean Paul de Marchi, architect; Norman McGrath, Christopher H. L. Owen, architect. 40: Emmett Bright, Rome, Howard Dilday, ar-chitect. 41: John Martinez. 42: Fil Hunter. 44-47: Eduino J. Pereira from Arts & Words. 49-53: William J. Hennessy Jr. 54-61: Elsie J. Hennig. 62-67: William J. Hennessy Jr. 68: Fil Hunter. 71: Arezou Katoozian. 72-75: Frederic F. Bigio from B-C Graphics. 77-87: John Massey. 88-95: Frederic F. Bigio from B-C Graphics. 96, 97: Elsie J. Hennig. 98, 99: Arezou Katoozian. 100-107: Walter Hilmers Jr. from HJ Commericial Art. 109-115: William J. Hennessy Jr. 116: Fil Hunter. 118, 119: Eduino J. Pereira from Arts & Words. 120-123: John Massey. 124, 125: Arezou Katoozian. 126-133: Frederic F. Bigio from B-C Graphics.

Acknowledgments

The index/glossary for this book was prepared by Louise Hedberg. The editors also wish to thank the following: Glen C. Baker, Contractor, Alexandria, Va.; Albert A. Barden III, Maine Wood Heat Co., Norridgewock, Me.; Walter Bazer, The Fireplace Center, Rockville, Md.; C. Crouch Jr., Arlington Public Schools Career Center, Arlington, Va.; The Fireplace Mantel Shop, Kensington, Md.; Gary Fletcher, Brick Institute of America, McLean, Va.; Mike Flynn, Preference Contractors, Jessup, Md.; Jack Glass, Brick Association of North Carolina, Greensboro, N.C.; Willie L. Glenn, Triangle Brick Company, Durham, N.C.; Tim Glidden, Resource Policy Center, Thayer School of Engineering, Dartmouth College, Han-over, N.H.; Home Energy Digest, Minneapolis, Minn.; Jack T. Irwin, Inc., Rockville, Md.; Edward Kegley and James B. Mock, L. C. Smith, Inc., Alexandria, Va.; Ronald Mazzeo, Mazzeo's Chimney Services and Sales, Rockland, Me.; J.P. Moran III, Jo-Moco Products Co., Tulsa, Okla.; Stephen H. Morris, Vermont Castings, Inc., Randolph, Vt.; Bill Morrison, IXL, Inc., Greensboro, N.C.; National Forest Products Association, Washington, D.C.; National Museum of American History, Division of Domestic Life, The Smithsonian Institution, Washington, D.C.; National Trust for Historic Preservation, Washington, D.C.; Presley Development Co., Ahwatukee, House of the Future, Phoenix, Ariz.; Preway, Inc., Wis-consin Rapids, Wis.; Andrew and Thomas Raycroft, Rooftop Chimney Sweeps, Ltd., Alexandria, Va.; Tourne Shipman, The Firebox Buck Stove & Fan Co., Alexandria, Va.; Professor E. L. Stone, Soil Science Department, University of Florida, Gainsville, Fla.; Antonio Troiano Tile and Marble Co., Inc., Beltsville, Md.; Washington Stove Works, Everett, Wash.; Eugene Wengert, Wood Technology Department, Virginia Polytechnic Institute & Virginia State University, Blacksburg, Va.; Professor Richard Wilson, Division of Architectural History, University of Virginia, Charlottesville, Va.; Don Yonker, Fairfax, Va. The editors also thank Alexander S. Heard, Edgar Henry and Wendy Murphy, writers, for their help with this book.

Index/Glossary

Printed in U.S.A.